Homeschool

Like an

Expert

ANNE
CROSSMAN

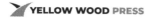

 YELLOW WOOD PRESS

Endorsements

Overwhelmed parents rejoice—this is the resource you have been hoping to find. Whether you are emergency schooling or want to know how to homeschool better, there is no better guide than *Homeschool Like an Expert*. If parents want to take their child's home education—and their college readiness—seriously, this resource is where they should start. Anne Crossman offers a perspective on homeschooled education I haven't seen anywhere else—she really has sat at every chair at the table. *Homeschool Like an Expert* is an excellent guide that is a must-read for all parents looking to teach their children at home. It is a practical, smart, much-needed resource that should be read by homeschooling families everywhere.

"DEAN SUE" WASIOLEK, Senior Advisor in Student Affairs, Duke University

Homeschool Expert gives timely, relevant insights derived from personal experience and extensive research. As Director of Admissions at OSU helping students from all backgrounds transition to college, I highly recommend *Homeschool Like an Expert* as a guide. You'll get an engaging, thought-provoking honesty designed to help you make the right decision for you and your family.

NOAH BUCKLEY, Director of Admissions, Oregon State University

As the founder of a homeschooling company, I've met a lot of folks writing about homeschooling — there is simply no one like Anne. Her resources are the culmination of decades of academic study, firsthand experience, and coaching other homeschooling families to distill her treasure trove of knowledge into a gift every family can learn from. There's really nothing else like it.

RYAN DELK, CEO Primer

If you want just one accessible, all-encompassing, empowering guide to homeschooling for success, here it is. Anne Crossman has experience and empathy in spades. She'll answer your questions, point you to the right resources, calm your fears, quell your doubts, and get your homeschool up and running in no time. *Homeschool Like an Expert* is the fast-track to homeschool success for your family.

DEBRA BELL, PHD, Executive Director, Aim Online Academy, author of *The Ultimate Guide to Homeschooling Teens*

I wish Homeschool Expert had been available when Sandi and I began to homeschool our four sons in the early 1980s. Anne has authored a well-thought-out resource for any parent embarking on the wonderful journey of learning together as a family.

STEVE DEMME, Founder, Math-U-See, Building Faith Families

For such a time as this—we need a book just like this one. Here is a one-stop guide for families struggling to adjust to the new educational realities. If you are an eager learn-at-homer or a reluctant how-can-I-survivor, you will find this book an invaluable help. And (one day!) your kids will be grateful, too, as they realize how well you have prepared them for what comes next.

PETER FEAVER, Professor of Political Science, Duke University

Homeschool Like an Expert is a must-read for any family that is considering or has already decided to embark on this exciting journey. The book offers easy-to-follow tools and strategies, and answers so many of the questions that those new to homeschooling will encounter. Anne's style is easy to follow, and it feels like you are having a conversation with a friend who has already blazed the trail for a successful homeschooling experience. This book should be the first stop in your homeschooling journey.

PATRICIA SCHETTER, Professor in MIND Institute at University of California, Davis, author of *Homeschooling the Child with Autism*

For you

Publisher's Cataloging-in-Publication Data
provided by Five Rainbows Cataloging Services

Names: Crossman, Anne, author.

Title: Homeschool like an expert / Anne Crossman.

Description: Bend, OR : Yellow Wood Press, 2020. | Includes index.

Identifiers: ISBN 978-1-7355441-0-6 (paperback) | ISBN 978-1-7355441-1-3 (ebook)

Subjects:
   LCSH: Home schooling. | Home schooling–Handbooks, manuals, etc. | Education–
   Parent participation. | Parenting. | Education. | BISAC: EDUCATION / Home Schooling.
   | EDUCATION / Parent Participation.

Classification: LCC LC40 .C76 2020 (print) | LCC LC40 (ebook) | DDC 371.04/2--dc23.

Contents

Foreword

OVERWHELMED PARENTS REJOICE.

This resource is what you have been hoping to find. Whether you are emergency schooling or want to know how to homeschool better, there is no better guide than *Homeschool Like an Expert*.

Deciding to homeschool is a big step, and wise parents will pursue expert help as they try to locate the right resources and strategically balance a robust academic education with the personal and social development of their children. There's a lot to consider.

I've been working with students at Duke University for the past 40 years, largely as the Dean of Students, and in the last two decades as an Associate Vice President for Student Affairs. This year, I was named Senior Advisor in Student Affairs. In addition, for the past 7 years, I have served as a faculty-in-residence, living in a residence hall with 190 first-year students. Frankly, it has been a joy. I've seen some students arrive for their freshman year well prepared and others not at all.

If parents want to take their child's home education—and their college readiness—seriously, this resource is where they should start. Anne Crossman offers a perspective on homeschooled education I haven't seen anywhere else—she really has sat at every chair at the table. She was homeschooled for six years during elementary and junior high, back when homeschooling was just getting started. As a freshman, she transitioned successfully into her local public high school, where she rose to the top in athletics and student leadership, graduating as valedictorian. From there she went on to Stanford University and Duke University.

Anne could have gone on to a high paying career, but instead chose education—becoming a teacher in public high schools and later on military bases in

South Korea. When she realized that the tools she had developed for her high school students could be extended to help her enlisted soldier students, Anne began to publish best-selling books on practical education, starting with *Getting the Best Out of College* and *Study Smart, Study Less.*

Her experience came full circle when she made four books and four babies in the same eight year timespan and began homeschooling her children, customizing what she had developed for high school students and enlisted soldiers for her kids. Over the next 13 years, Anne continued to equip herself, applying and adapting all her classroom training into homeschool tutoring, and seeking expertise on how to support students with learning preferences and special learning needs when two of her children were diagnosed. Since then, she has consulted for many new homeschool families, guiding them through the process of teaching from home and improving their current homeschooling set-up.

With all this in her back pocket, Anne had intended to publish this book in 2022 with a large publisher, as her other books had been. But, when COVID-19 began to affect families and the education of children across the nation, she set aside that ambition to make this resource available to families immediately.

For those unaccustomed to the publishing world, there is a lot more that goes into releasing a book than just writing it (which is an undertaking itself!) I respect Anne for choosing the road less traveled, giving up the opportunity to print this book with a major publisher so she could help families quickly.

Homeschool Like an Expert is an excellent guide that is a must-read for all parents looking for a practical way to educate their children at home. It is a practical, smart, much-needed resource that should be read by homeschooling families everywhere.

"DEAN SUE" WASIOLEK, Duke University

Acknowledgements

The catalyst that brought the need for this book to public awareness is nothing to celebrate.

COVID-19 has been hard on families in many ways. While developing a homeschool resource to support parents as teachers (which they could adapt to almost any curriculum or teaching format) has long been an ambition of mine, what led us to this need becoming wide-scale so quickly is sobering.

So, first, thank you to the parents and teachers who have exemplified flexibility, creativity, long-suffering, and resilience in continuing to do your utmost to provide for the holistic well-being of children during this season.

Untold hours by a team of unnamed people are invested into creating a project of this magnitude. It is the very least I can do to thank as many as possible for making *Homeschool Like an Expert* (both the book and video series) possible.

Before thanking anyone else, I want to first thank my husband, Josh. I won't go into the mushy sentiments here that none of you care to read—about him carrying with me my ambitions that, at times, felt like a backpack of rocks rather than wings. Nor will I belabor the point by explaining that, as my chief investor, partner, and unpaid media intern, had Josh not sacrificed time, work, sleep, finances, exercise, and all downtime by picking up my slack and helping me develop this resource, I could never have built Homeschool Expert in time to help families educate their children during COVID. Instead, I will simply say: Thank you, Josh, for helping me help others.

By extension, Team Crossman—Evangeline, Evelyn, Isaiah, and Josiah—you are incredible. Thank you for your patience, extra Mom-jobs, encouragement, and prayers. And, for baking me cookies and chocolate cakes, and creating many-sticky-note-love-drawings along the way. You inspire me. Blessings over each of you in your own journeys.

Oddly enough, I want to acknowledge the miserable situation that prompted my Mom to homeschool me; good can come from bad, even though we wish the bad had never happened in the first place. To my parents—thank you for having the courage to ignore the nay-sayers and for daring to teach me at home. The best parts of my childhood were at home with you, and I treasure our wealth of times together.

From there, the team expands significantly. Thank you to "Dean Sue" Wasiolek for partnering with me to unveil the mystery of the university's perspective of homeschoolers and to support this project in many ways. Thank you to Bryn Mooth for editing this book with professionalism, skill, and a sense of humor, finding creative ways to make the deadline work. Thank you to Victoria Kelly for collaborating with me on op-eds to get words of encouragement and help out to families when it was most needed. Thank you to Dr. Debra Bell, Noah Buckley, Ryan Delk, Steve Demme, Dr. Peter Feaver, and Patricia Schetter, for generously lending your name and voice to support this project. And, thank you to my team of experts who graciously shared their stories, their time, their feedback, and their ideas: Lonnie Bang, Autumn Bonner, Becky Bonner, Bob Bonner, Danielle Burkholder, Perry Burkholder, Tara Chandlee, Heather Craig, F. Ann Crossman, Steve Crossman, Cindy Ditman, Nikki Eisenhut, Kim Esbenshade, Bruce Fidler, Carol Fidler, Kyle Hickey, David Hobbet, Cara Hopkins, John Hopkins, Susan Hutchins, Rebecca Ifland, Julie Kayser, Jenny Lee, Stacy Manning, Beverly McCord, Kellee Metty, Allie Meyer, Ben Patterson, Cece Phillips, Micah Rowland, Mike Smith, and Ann Sumner.

In addition, there is the behind the scenes team that made *Homeschool Like an Expert: Video Series*, website, or book possible: Tanner and Colette Boley with Fox Hollow Creative, Kaelin McDowell as stylist, FaceOut in saving the day with a fire-drill of visual aids, Metaleap Creative in doing all that your name says, and Pinkston Group and MuteSix for getting these tools into the hands of families who needed it most. No more late night texts from me, I promise. Thank you for responding to the need (bravely risking a ridiculous deadline to do so) and launching Homeschool Expert well.

Introduction

YOU CAN DO THIS—AND YOU ARE NOT ALONE.

Consider me a friend. These chapters represent many wonderful conversations ahead of us, inspired by evergreen questions parents have asked for decades about homeschooling.

Whether or not you decide to homeschool your kids by the end of this book, you'll get no judgement from me. Too many conversations with friends about homeschooling have begun with them saying, "I'm such a bad parent because I don't homeschool my kids," or "I'm afraid I am going to ruin my kid's education because I'm not doing this right," or "Homeschooling looks too hard, I could never be home with my kids all day."

So, let's start fresh. We all love our kids; homeschooling does not define how much we love them. And nobody is earning secret superstar-parent-badges for teaching kids at home. Furthermore, if we keep seeking out resources and asking for help, we aren't going to ruin our children's lives; instead, we are going to model for them what it means to learn, challenge ourselves, grab tools to do something new, and adapt to change.

There are a lot of ways to get a great education. I actually experienced quite a few of them as a student, a collegian, and a professional educator in military barracks, colleges, and around kitchen tables for the past 20 years. What I have learned is that learning is not one-size-fits-all.

As a public high school teacher, I did my very best to impact all 120 of my students every day. But even on my best days as a teacher—when I worked far more hours than I was paid (I earned about $2 an hour at one point) and did my utmost to inspire and encourage every student who walked through my door—it was never enough to reach them all.

My colleagues lamented the same challenge.

Our hearts were in the right place, but sheer effort was not enough to overcome the significant obstacles we faced in reaching our full roster every period. We were daily handed rows of students coming out of rugged backgrounds, family needs, hunger, exhaustion, anxiety, and depression—and being asked to work miracles in 40 minutes with all 30 of them at once. As a former teacher, I have high respect for those called to the field of public education as a vocation. That I chose to homeschool my children is not a critique of the system but rather a recognition of what I saw in my own classroom—that 1:1 can be an ideal way to learn.

As for which is harder, homeschool or homework, my vote is actually on the latter. I have the utmost respect for friends who send their kids to school all day and get them back at 3:00, only to have to shuttle them to activities and supervise them finishing homework. That sounds painfully difficult; few education hurdles are harder than teaching a worn-out student at the end of the day. My job looks easy by comparison, where I get my students fresh in the morning and by lunch we are done with the hard stuff.

We all love our kids; homeschooling does not define how much we love them.

When I was a student, each of my school environments challenged and grew me in different ways. Reflecting back, I remember when chemistry was a terrible fit with one teacher, and the following semester how a new teacher took the same subject from monochrome to living color. When the right peer group transformed a burdensome group assignment into a glittering opportunity to explore, create, and stretch ourselves beyond what we thought was possible. And when personal grief made learning at home the very safest and best place to be—free from ridicule, free to love learning, free to explore the world from my library and dream about someday seeing it for myself.

I was homeschooled for six years up until eighth grade, then attended private school for a year before transitioning as a freshman into our local public high school. From there, I went on to Stanford and Duke universities. While private, public, and Montessori school all added value to my educational journey, homeschooling taught me to be driven, self-motivated, and independent, and prepared me more for college and my career than any other part of my education.

Where I saw my peers at Stanford and Duke struggle to develop their own systems and schedules for managing workloads, I was ahead of the game. I kept it a secret from my professors that I had been homeschooled—at the time, there were some unfortunate assumptions that went along with that word. Inevitably, my professors would commend my diligence in attending office hours, my self-discipline at completing assignments early, or my creative and unique approaches to projects. Then, I would tell them my secret. It was marvelous to sit through their gasps of surprise; to respond, "Yes, really" to their questioning; to be a new datapoint in academia as some of the first generation of homeschoolers coming of college age.

Since then, I have had the opportunity to publish my first book, *Getting the Best Out of College,* with a professor and dean from Duke University. At one point in writing the book, Dean Sue Wasiolek and I dove further into researching what university admissions directors thought of homeschooled applicants. In the course of our interviews with deans from other elite universities, it became apparent that perspectives about homeschooled college applicants was changing and that there were clear suggestions about how homeschooled students could improve their applications. We finalized our research in 2020 and it is published in full, for the first time, in Chapter 14.

But I'm getting ahead of myself. Let's back up and ask the critical first question: So, where should parents start?

Many who are new to homeschooling feel lost in the overwhelming sea of resources, alone in the unknowns, unclear about lingo and differences in teaching methods, and uncertain if they are even doing it "right." Too many have felt unqualified to teach when they were perfectly capable of meeting their child's educational needs—they just needed some tools to make it doable. The chapter titles of this book honor the many parents who opened their homes and educational journeys to me, asking the concerned, thoughtful, chapter-heading questions that led me to write this book.

You don't need my education or background to homeschool your children— you just need the tools and advice I have developed, with the help of over 100 experts and successful parent teachers, for my family and yours.

School is more than curriculum. It is more than a peer group. It is more than a building and a bell schedule and a bus route. Sometimes we make school out to be something bigger and harder than it needs to be. It is a space to grow and learn and discover; an opportunity to fail and succeed; a season for self-discovery, self-motivation, and learning about others. It is a place to identify our weaknesses and strengths and support both of them uniquely so we can holistically grow, do, and be.

All of this is possible in school; but just because it is possible doesn't mean it is happening.

Politics, economics, educators, family dynamics, health issues, job changes, and district boundary lines all play a part in what school has become. For some students, the traditional school model is a place to thrive; for others, it is a barrier.

The aim of this book is to make a great education accessible to everyone. No matter where you live, how much money you make, who you know, or what you know, as parents it is possible to give your kids a great education. *Homeschool Like an Expert* maps out the means to provide a customized education for your child with excellence, distilling teaching principles into practical tools I learned as a professional educator to enlisted soldiers, high school students, ESL students, and students with special needs—not to mention skills I adapted for myself in my own homeschool environment all the way through college. Whether you are new to homeschooling or looking to take homeschool to the next level, this book will give you the practical tools and expert help you need to become the best teacher you can be.

I Need to Start Homeschooling Next Week—Is That Possible?

Quick Start Guide to Homeschooling

W hat do you get when you have a third grader, a sixth grader, and a full work-load all stuck at home under quarantine?

Sadly, this is not a joke.

At the time of writing this chapter, the US was grounded due to COVID-19. Except for outings for food and medical care, most Americans were required to stay home. All of that was relevant to this chapter as 54 million students nationwide found themselves becoming something they never imagined: homeschoolers. Equally challenged were the parents who discovered overnight that they have become teachers. Even after COVID-19 is a distant memory, surprises in life will still arise. Whether a job relocation, family tragedy, or an unexpected student need, families will still find themselves needing to homeschool in a hurry.

Believe it or not, I was in a similar season years ago—where the goal was to just get through the next 12 months as effectively as possible. Many of the tools in this chapter were developed the hard way, by adapting what I knew about homeschooling with excellence to meet our family's needs during a challenging season. I learned how to pare things down to the bare minimum so I could do those well.

In twenty years of teaching, my students were on honor roll, autistic, fresh from prison, college-bound, and pregnant teens, not to mention homeschooling my four children since 2006. In all of these settings, what mattered most was the ability to customize the content to the need of each student. While this book is loaded with extensive helps that will transform homeschoolers from survive to thrive, this chapter focuses on a quick start guide that will give you four tools to create homeschool sanity in one afternoon. Along with those four tools, this chapter lays out how to homeschool legally within the school district and some easy curriculum guidance so you are first-day-ready in very little time.

FLEXIBLE STRUCTURES

Whether you are planning to homeschool for a month during your life change or a full school year, what will make this transition easiest for all involved is super clear expectations. In other words, write them down. Prison studies, military protocol, educational paradigms, and coaches for special needs students all have at least one principle in common—structure creates a clear purpose, a sense of calm, and an effective way to accomplish a goal together. Sometimes the surprise changes in our lives may make us feel a little trapped. Why not learn from others who have felt limited by circumstance, need, or geography to see how they overcame?

Once structures are in place, reward them with play. Without play, work wouldn't happen. (Let's be honest...would you respond to emails at 11:30pm if you thought you were never getting another weekend, paycheck, or kudos? Why would our kids be any different?) The key is to balance the size and frequency of incentives with the job done so it doesn't break the bank or lose its shine. I recognize the topic of incentivizing children can be a sensitive one—in our family, children are expected to do their school and chores because they are valuable members of our team; work is not optional. But, play is also an intentional part of our lives. Carrots can be just as powerful as sticks, and in seasons of surprise upheaval a few well-placed carrots will go a long way to establishing a new routine, which will lead to a sense of calm, which will help everyone move past carrots and sticks and stress.

TOOL ONE: STUDENT GOALS

We all do better when we know what's expected of us. Kids are no different. Type up a set of student goals to have your child read aloud each morning. Feel free to use mine if that makes it easier. (You can also print them out free at *Links to Experts* on HomeschoolExpert.com).

Notice that these are all "do" statements. If I tell you "Don't scratch your nose" and wait 30 seconds...your nose will likely start to feel itchy. So, instead of telling a child "Don't bang your head on the desk," say "Sit with a quiet body." Reading this aloud each morning establishes a game plan and makes the goals clear—which is especially helpful to return to at any point in the day if things aren't going as you hoped. Draw a smiley face as your child meets each goal, and put a sticker on his calendar if he meets all his smileys as well as completing assignments for the day.

Extra Student Goals

I promise to work my best with a good attitude.

 Sit with a quiet body, head up

 Respect personal space

 Focus & smile

 Treat supplies with respect

Positive feedback—even as small as a sticker or a smiley face—is necessary to developing momentum. Older students , of course, may not be won over by clip art and stickers but will still benefit from having age-appropriate goals established, and to feel seen and recognized when you sign off their calendar as they meet their goals daily. So, decide what meets your student's emotional and academic needs best.

Once momentum is achieved, feedback and incentives can be scaled back and become less frequent. In the beginning, if your student thinks the sticker is prize enough, go with that...start small. However, if you have an older student or a challenging set-up and a larger incentive is needed, consider these. Each sticker earns 10 extra minutes of tech time; or every ten stickers earns a special family movie night. Or, go bigger—20 stickers earns a pony. Well, maybe not a pony.

Part of the fun is brainstorming together what a good incentive might be for accomplishing student goals for five days (which, by the way, might take more than a week to reach at first.) Remember: grace is needed in times of transition—for your student and especially for you—so don't make it too hard in the beginning. It's better to have some early wins initially and build momentum than to crush all sense of hope and possibility by demanding the unattainable.

TOOL TWO: THE TIME LADDER

What would an ideal day look like to you? A time ladder is a great way to picture your whole day at a glance and give structure without rigidity—especially for children who are new to time management or for whom an hour of worksheets can feel like an eternity.

Our ladder begins at 7am with bullet points to the side of what is expected at the start of the day. After that we have Morning Meeting (where we sit down to discuss the day ahead) and the page continues from there. Kids who show up at the table dressed, fed, and ready for the day at Morning Meeting earn dessert that afternoon—which has been a significant enough incentive for my kids. To the left of the column is a section for "if extra time" and a list of possibilities my children could choose if they are ahead of the game that day, such as practice piano, kitchen chores, pet care, or play outside. That said, your time is not my time; your kids are not my kids; your time ladder is not my time ladder. I encourage you to use the principles of this time ladder and apply it to your own family's needs and schedule.

The beauty of this routine versus a timetable (which tells you to eat breakfast at 8:30, wash dishes at 9, and start math worksheets at 9:15) is flexibility. If it is 9:15 and you still aren't done with breakfast, just keep working down the ladder rather than living by a stopwatch. [Insert a sigh of relief here.] The idea is to build a dependable, attainable routine and post it where the kids can see it.

Some homeschooling consultants recommend starting with math, or your hardest subject, at the beginning of every school day. For us, that didn't work. We found that starting with journaling for five minutes was an easy onramp to the day. Some of my students struggled with anxiety challenges, so after journals those students would often complete their work in the exact order every day as a way of promoting calm. Other students did well by choosing which core subjects to complete first as it fit their mood that day. Flexibility between students is a beautiful thing, so figure out what works best for your student and your family. However you decide to order your core subjects, blocking out time

Time Ladder

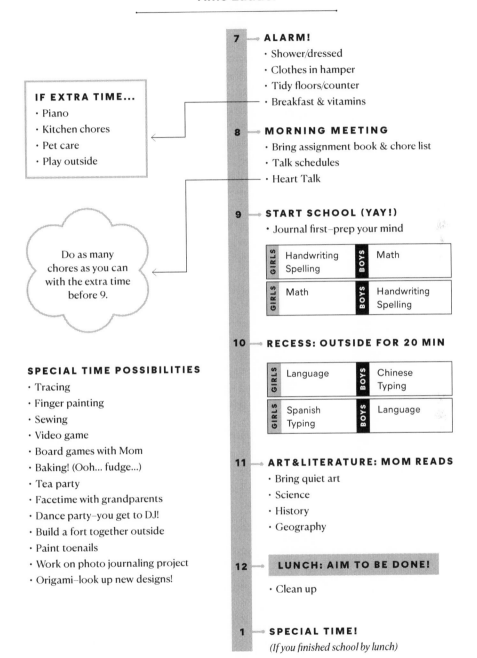

7 — **ALARM!**
- Shower/dressed
- Clothes in hamper
- Tidy floors/counter
- Breakfast & vitamins

IF EXTRA TIME...
- Piano
- Kitchen chores
- Pet care
- Play outside

8 — **MORNING MEETING**
- Bring assignment book & chore list
- Talk schedules
- Heart Talk

Do as many chores as you can with the extra time before 9.

9 — **START SCHOOL (YAY!)**
- Journal first–prep your mind

GIRLS		BOYS	
Handwriting Spelling		Math	
Math		Handwriting Spelling	

SPECIAL TIME POSSIBILITIES
- Tracing
- Finger painting
- Sewing
- Video game
- Board games with Mom
- Baking! (Ooh... fudge...)
- Tea party
- Facetime with grandparents
- Dance party–you get to DJ!
- Build a fort together outside
- Paint toenails
- Work on photo journaling project
- Origami–look up new designs!

10 — **RECESS: OUTSIDE FOR 20 MIN**

GIRLS		BOYS	
Language		Chinese Typing	
Spanish Typing		Language	

11 — **ART&LITERATURE: MOM READS**
- Bring quiet art
- Science
- History
- Geography

12 — **LUNCH: AIM TO BE DONE!**
- Clean up

1 — **SPECIAL TIME!**
(If you finished school by lunch)

with clear expectations enables everyone to get their work done more efficiently.

It is critical to note at this point that less time is needed to practice a subject with 1:1 attention than it does in a class of 1:30. A significant part of a traditional class day is devoted to, what we teachers call, "transitions" such as getting students seated and on task, passing out and collecting papers, explaining directions multiple times, and so on—which is why it is possible for homeschoolers to finish the same amount of work in less time.

The general plan is this: aim to work on math, reading, and writing 5 days a week for 15-20 minutes each. Then, aim to work on science and history 2-3 days a week for about 15-20 minutes. Please note, these times are just an estimate. In the beginning, when your student is adapting to your new role as teacher, a math lesson may take 40 minutes that later in the year might take less than half that. There is definitely an adjustment period. That said, homeschooling is less concerned with time spent at the table, and more focused on mastery of the content.

Also realize that just because I say "math 5 days a week," doesn't really mean five days. Many traditional schools offer block scheduling, where 5 days' worth of math is accomplished in three school days—especially at the high school level. Your curriculum will map out an appropriate number of lessons a week, and it is up to you to organize those lessons where it makes the most sense for you.

Be sure to build a recess into your routine, pausing between subjects for a 5 minute chore break, and then once an hour for 15-20 minutes of outside playtime and maybe a snack. We tend to go with the routine of school/chore, school/recess, school/chore, school/lunch— that way, by lunch, most of the schoolwork and housework is underway.

Looking ahead, there are four ways to educate at home (which we discuss in Chapter Two in greater depth.) If you have chosen Private Homeschooling you will have the most autonomy and creativity in building your school schedule to adapt to your lifestyle.

For our family, if the kids finish all their core subjects by noon, we have Special Time after lunch. Whether we have nowhere to go but the grocery or an afternoon full of outings it helps to get the work done quickly so we have more time to play (and so math worksheets don't drag on foreeeeveeer...). Special Time could be as short as 15 minutes, depending on the age group—but knowing it's there helps us push through the multiplication tables.

There is Wow Power by giving an activity a sparkly name, and calling it Special Time has made it feel even more special. Just make sure you don't give away the reward of Special Time if they haven't earned it, otherwise your magic wand will become a dud.

Special Time

- Tea Party
- Card Games (*Spoons, Go Fish, Old Maid, Hearts*)
- Board Games
- Tracing
- Finger Painting
- Stitchery (*mending, crochet, cross-stitch, knitting, sewing*)
- Video Game Tournament
- Baking
- Facetime with Relatives
- Dance Party
- Build a Fort
- Paint Toenails
- Build a Photo Journal
- Origami–Look up new designs
- Perler Beads
- Toothpick Structures
- Charades
- Sock Basketball
- Sock Hockey
- Hide and Seek
- Sardines
- Indoor Balance Beam
- The Floor is Lava
- Treasure Hunt
- Topple Dominos
- Capture the Flag
- Four Square
- Jump Rope
- Marbles/Jacks
- Pictionary
- Pitching Pennies
- Indoor Bowling
- Balloon Volleyball
- Family Photo Game

TOOL THREE: THE ASSIGNMENT CALENDAR

Print out a freebie month at a glance, or pick one up at the dollar store. This is where you will write your student's assignments for the week so she can keep herself accountable to her work, checking off each assignment as she completes it. If life has truly caught you by surprise and you don't have schoolwork to give your students while you wait for the curriculum to arrive, here are a few suggestions (which you can modify by age).

Start with the 3 R's each day (Reading, Writing, and Arithmetic...I know, it's a terrible title, since the R's are in the wrong places, but that's what it's historically called). Journaling for 5-10 minutes a day is an excellent way for your student to hone his writing skills, not to mention a healthy place to work through his feelings about the new normal. Even if he can't write, he can dictate and you can play scribe. Free-writing is a valuable exercise on its own, but if he hits writer's block look up "free journal prompts for junior high" or whatever grade level you need for some quick ideas.

For math, everyone can be faster at addition, subtraction, multiplication, division, squares, and square root tables—so, practice those with a timer and flashcards. Find ways to make a game of it. Literature is even easier, with libraries in almost every city and free downloadable eBooks and audiobooks from most libraries through Libby and Overdrive—Caldecott winners are a great place to start. Look up poems online by Shel Silverstein, Edgar Allen Poe, Billy Collins, and Maya Angelou and read one aloud every day. Then, ask your kids to write something with the same poetic music to it; they will likely amaze you. If all you accomplish the first week is writing, math, and reading—and practicing your student goals and time ladder as you go—count that as a win. Even for the first month, if your students are elementary age.

Even though it is your right as a parent to school how you choose, there is protocol to follow depending on the state where you live.

In the beginning, learning to homeschool is more than just learning subjects at home—it is learning how to work together in entirely new roles. Of course, stretch these guidelines as much as you need given the situation you face. I have known some families who had to homeschool in a hurry because of tragedy—a parent died and the kids were too stressed to go to school for the rest of the school year; or, a child was in an accident and needed to remain at home for the rest of the school year to recover; or, a second grader was choked twice in one day by the same student so her parents removed her from school for a few weeks until the district could relocate the offender to a more appropriate school setting. When life is hard, school can wait. Sometimes just doing a couple subjects a day to establish a sense of routine, calm, and normalcy is all you need—and then just read great books aloud, go outside, and discover your city together.

Oodles of studies have been published showing the positive mental health benefits of being able to control and manage time. What a great opportunity to give your kids that same sense of control and freedom in their education by learning how to manage their time during this season.

Should you be in a place where you want to move past the 3 R's and you are still waiting for curriculum to arrive, consider adding these to your routine. Merge art with geography by making a collage or printing out free maps of other countries to color, label, and discuss. And then there is spelling—free lists abound online if you search for "free spelling lists for grade ___." Twelve words a week, copied 2-3 times a day, will go far. There are also great free typing games online to help your student improve in speed and accuracy. And, for sure, now's the time to google "science experiments you can do in your kitchen" and see what happens.

Aim to set aside 20 minutes per student at the start of each week to organize their schedules and set-aside materials. (I recommend not trying to look up printables with your class waiting at the kitchen table...it will be like herding cats to get them back when you are ready.) Organizing the student calendars will require the most time and effort of the four tools, but it's worth it. The kids love the sense of accomplishment as they cross off what they have completed each day, and it makes keeping everyone on track that much easier. When the day is done, put a sticker on it. Castaways and POW's have all had their way of etching survival hash marks to buoy their spirits. Your kids (and you!) need it too.

Finally, the calendar is a great place to post chores (see page 221) —and, not just cleaning their own room. Helping the household gives children a sense of ownership, confidence, and self-reliance, and makes them feel like a valuable part of the team. My kids have been unloading dishwashers since the age of 4, doing dishes at age 6, their own laundry at 7, and baking/making meals for the family at 11—just to mention a few. All with adult guidance, of course.

In the beginning it was significantly *more* work on my part to teach them to clean the bathroom than it was to clean it myself—but now I have four kids who can all clean a bathroom properly, and I can honestly say it was totally worth it. Each of our kids have a list of household chores they are responsible for every week, and we divide up the house for cleaning days weekly. Don't be afraid to turn off tech and make your living space a place you can be proud to share.

TOOL FOUR: REWARD YOURSELF

Make time to dream with your kids during this transition. Spend a mealtime coming up with a bucket list of fun ideas for the season—like family game nights, roasting s'mores in the broiler, DIY projects, or drive-through DQ Blizzards— and put it on your calendar. Planning fun gives everyone something to look forward to and helps offset anxiety.

MAKE SURE YOU ARE LEGAL

Please, oh please, don't start homeschooling until you have officially registered as a homeschooler with your district. Even though it is your right as a parent to school how you choose, there is protocol to follow depending on the state where you live. If you are pulling your child from a public school setting to transition to homeschooling, the easiest first step is to contact the counseling department at your child's school and ask if someone there can walk you through the proper steps or direct you to the right person. If they don't know where to direct you, or if you are leaving a private school, contact your school district and ask for the person who oversees homeschool registration. You can also visit Homeschool-Expert.com and look for "Links to Experts" for quick connections to your state's requirements and resources.

Typically, each school district has staff dedicated to making sure home-schoolers register, have access to district resources as needed, and are in compliance with state requirements. Enrolling in the fall is sometimes as easy as mailing in a one-page form to the district office. But, if you are pulling out mid-year, it may be best to start by working with the school directly about transitioning out of the system. Make sure you have also looked up your state's requirements for homeschooling—many states insist the parent teacher has a high school diploma, GED, or equivalent test scores, so it's worth checking ahead of time.

STREAMLINE CURRICULUM

As I mentioned earlier in this chapter, if you find yourself in an especially stress-ful life transition, look for ways to keep school simple. Locating a math text, an English textbook which incorporates writing, and a reading list that naturally incorporates an historical or scientific element is a great start until you get your bearings. It is totally fine to stay with the basics for a little while and add more later. (Remember, this is the Quick Start Guide—a more in-depth conversation about curriculum is in Chapter 8.)

There are ways to creatively combine subjects into a block format, much like what you see in traditional schools, to check off state goals for two subjects using one assignment. Your state's education standards are available online if you research "education standards for ____ state grade ___", and I suspect once you get through the jargon you will find it to be very doable.

For example, I know of one state that required students at the 4th grade level to read a biography in History class, study a groundbreaking discovery in DNA for Science, and write a 5 paragraph persuasive essay for English in the second semester. All three state standards were satisfied by reading a single book about Rosalind Franklin and writing an essay about why her name should be routinely coupled with Watson and Crick. Less can be more.

Most homeschool families I know with average students accomplish all the state standards by spring; and those families with students who qualify for an

Individualized Education Plan (IEP) have different standards. Reading your state's standards will help you simplify your year by first understanding what is required.

Some states require that you teach a certain list of subjects throughout the year. Please note, they are not necessarily asking you to teach all those subjects *every day*, or even every week—some can be organized on a block schedule, such as health, where you focus on it for a month or two during the year alongside your core subjects.

Also important to note is that if your state has a required list of subjects, that does not necessarily mean you must purchase curriculum in that subject. If it is easiest for you to purchase a block of readymade curriculum and lesson plans, go for it. Or, if your budget is constrained you can address that subject using free online or library resources. So, read your state's requirements carefully and don't feel like you have to require more of yourself than is required by the state.

Part of streamlining curriculum is paring down. Did you know that most grammar and math curriculums include not only the core content but additional exercises so teachers can assign extra work if needed? It's a revelation for most homeschool parents in their first year or two to discover that they don't have to complete every problem on the page. But, if you think back to high school math class, it was not uncommon for the teacher to assign "problems 1-20, odds" and have you skip the rest. Once your student has mastered the concept, move on—and make space for a little review here and there to maintain mastery.

On the other hand, if your student has completed all the problems on that topic and still

There are ways to creatively combine subjects into a block format, much like what you see in traditional schools, to check off state goals for two subjects using one assignment.

doesn't understand it, do not move to the next unit. Struggles can sometimes be an indicator that you need to switch curriculum, which we cover in Chapter 8, or in rare cases might indicate a learning disability, which we discuss in Chapter 11.

Find ways to utilize non-curricular resources—such as library DVD's, PBS episodes, or documentaries that expose students to core concepts, making learning easier when you sit down together. If Mom is leaving the kids with Nana while she is at work, this is a great time to drop them off with library DVD's that only require Nana to push play and that prep the students in the subject before they sit down to study with Mom later in the evening.

MATH

Last I checked there were 43 different homeschool math curriculums available just for grades 7 and 8. Yikes. I would encourage you not to get too creative when it comes to math. Look up homeschool curriculum fairs to see who are the most common vendors, reach out to your local online homeschool group asking what folks use, or read reviews for homeschool math online. Ultimately, look for a curriculum you can adapt to your child's learning preferences (which we dig into in Chapter 6) and that works at a pace that matches your child's strength in the subject.

As you look at various curricula, be sure to look for placement tests to decide which grade level is appropriate—some math programs offer them for free. Despite what seems obvious, grade 3 in one math curriculum is not the same as grade 3 in another. So, once you pick a curriculum you like, read the Table of Contents to determine what grade level your student actually needs. And, if you don't know, ask your student to talk through the Table of Contents with you to see what she knows. It is better to select a curriculum that is the best learning format for your child (and move her up or down a grade if needed) than to pick a curriculum that is a lesser fit but matches the grade you think she should be. In addition, if your student is between two grade levels, it is better to select the lower grade level and accelerate her through the program through whatever speed she requires than to risk creating gaps in her education by moving her to a grade level that is too advanced from the start.

You will quickly learn with homeschooling that one of the beauties of a custom education is that the grade level of the book you are using is not strictly important. More often than not, my kids have been in math books that were different from their official grade levels, and that tends to be the norm in the homeschool community. (It's one of the reasons many homeschooled students look a little lost if you ask them what grade they are in...because so many of the subjects are customized to the grade level they need.)

ENGLISH

English is a balancing act between reading, grammar, and writing. Depending on the curriculum, some programs weave reading, history, writing, grammar, and geography all into a singular program so that the subjects dovetail—which is my favorite way to learn. It makes history come alive for our children and consolidates our reading time into completing more subjects with less material. For students in transition, learning history through literature rather than a recounting of facts makes school easier to swallow—for the student and the parent teacher.

Don't be put off by the retail price of some of these great dovetailed curriculums, either. Some families buy used bundles on eBay, others buy the teacher guide from the publisher and look for the books at the library, and still others will save money by splitting the cost with another family to share resources by staggering start times. There are ethical work arounds, so don't let the sticker shock scare you away from a great curriculum.

YOU CAN DO THIS

I recognize this is a lot to take in—a bit like drinking from a fire hydrant. Once you have your four tools in place, you are official with the district, and you have the 3 R's figured out for the remainder of the year, it's going to get a whole lot easier. If you could use some extra encouragement at this point (can't we all?) look up local "homeschool co-ops" online and in social media groups to find homeschoolers in your community. Our homeschool co-ops have been a wonderful resource of friendship, ideas, and support—especially amidst COVID.

Ultimately, remember that homeschooling is more than finishing schoolwork at home. It is an opportunity to develop a self-motivated, responsible, creative learner. With the right balance of structure and flexibility, reward and restraint, chores and fun, you will be able to make the most of your transition. If there is one thing families discovered during COVID, it is that school can be something new, that there is more than one way to learn, and that home might be a great place to have school after all.

1

Why Do People Homeschool?

The Customized Education

Homeschooling is mysterious. What it really is and why people do it remains largely unknown to those outside the homeschool community for the simple reason that it happens around the privacy of our kitchen tables. *Homeschool Like an Expert* welcomes readers to come on in—sort of like an open house for homeschooling—showing how pursuing a great education at home can be doable for all families.

Many parents worry if homeschooling is affordable—it is. Many parents worry if they are capable of educating their children well—most are. Many parents worry that homeschooling their children will make them turn out awkward—they won't. There is so much more to homeschooling than most people realize, so come on in.

A LITTLE HISTORY

Before looking at how homeschooling is used today, let's briefly look at its role historically. (*Oh, right: This book was written by a teacher...it's starting with a history lesson. Figures.*)

One of the earliest reports of homeschooling appears in 800 BC, when historical records show Jewish fathers as the primary source of education for their sons. Continuing from there is evidence of Druid, Brahmin, Aztec, and Mayan cultures all teaching students through individualized instruction and home tutors. Shortly thereafter, records emerge in China of students who were tutored privately at home in preparation for the civil service examination. Homer later developed a concept of the ideal man being developed by his education, which led to fathers or tutors providing individualized education in homes of the upper classes in Greece, influencing theories of education for generations afterward.[1]

While it has gone by different names throughout history, homeschooling has been around for a long time. And for good reason: it works.

WHY DO PEOPLE HOMESCHOOL?

The National Center for Education Statistics (NCES) keeps tabs on education in the United States. At last count, there were 54 million students enrolled in American schools, 2.5 million of them being homeschooled. And in the last five years, the number of homeschooled students has increased by 17%. When the NCES asked parents why they chose to homeschool, the top three reasons parents listed were: concern about the safety or negative pressures of the school's environment (34%), dissatisfaction with the quality of schools (17%), and a desire to incorporate faith into instruction (14%).[2] So according to these statistics, people homeschool because they believe it offers a positive, quality learning environment that supports the beliefs of the family.

> In the beginning, even my dad was a little suspicious of home-schooling—until the results came back on our state exams in April, showing we were above grade level in all our subjects

As for my own history, my mom began teaching us at home in 1986 when it was barely legal to do so. I am immensely grateful to her. After two years in what should have been a solid elementary school, my parents discovered the toxic nature of my school environment and removed me at the end of the year.

"You changed after going to that school," my mom said to me, after reading the draft of this chapter. "Your dad frequently asked me, 'What happened to our happy little girl? She's just not as bubbly as she used to be.' We were both troubled by it and thought it could have been the school or the new baby or even that this was a normal part of growing up. We were new to parenting a school aged child and honestly were ignorant of what should have been clear warning signs. Even though it was a private school, the quality of the education was substandard and when you brought home worksheets I thought, 'I could do better than this.' The school was unwilling to give you more challenging work or address bullying behavior happening in your class." The only other school in our district was risky at best, which left Mom with homeschooling.

There were very few resources available to her in the beginning and no support groups; most families had to build their own curriculum from scratch. That plus the unsolicited advice she regularly got from relatives—that she was making square pegs for round holes and would ruin us for life—meant that it took nerves of steel to homeschool back in the day. (Thanks for hanging tough, Mom.) In the beginning, even my dad was a little suspicious of homeschooling—until the results came back on our state exams in April, showing we were above grade level in all our subjects and had improved beyond our former rate of growth. As kids, we were also happier than we had been. At that point, Dad became a strong advocate of homeschooling.

Now, of course, homeschooling is legal nationwide, lauded (and often desired) by colleges of their applicants, and well-supported with co-ops and almost a gluttony of curriculum choices. It's a whole new world.

STATISTIC NUMBER ONE

Homeschooling is not about withdrawing from the world because it is a scary place, or building a bubble around children to protect them from all pain. Or, at least, it isn't meant to be. The NCES recognizes that the greatest concern driving parents to homeschool is the safety or negative environment of the school. But that doesn't mean parents are pulling their kids out to lock them in a panic room until college—it means they are protecting or providing for them to the best of their ability.

By homeschooling their children, parents can temporarily remove some of the external variables that may distract from a holistic education when trying to grow love for learning, creativity, character, confidence, and a sense of place in the community. Children are malleable. It is standard practice over the course of a week for homeschool families to complete four or five mornings of school and then to fill their afternoons with sports, music lessons, theater classes, co-op extracurriculars, scout programs, field trips, cottage industries, martial arts, and more, largely with other homeschool families from 12-3pm.

As a result, many homeschool families find themselves overlapping at events and the social circle becomes personal; people feel known. The balance of adults to students during homeschool gatherings remains close, developing a tight-knit sense of community and the invaluable reference point of having other trustworthy adults present in our children's lives. It goes back to the time-worn adage, "It takes a village" proving true. Over time, personal growth and exposure to positive peer experiences make for strong young people who can then be exposed to more and more of the world with intentionality and resulting maturity.

One of the beautiful things about homeschooled children is their ability to naturally play or converse with a person of almost any age. One of the questions people new to this education model often ask is: What type of diversity do homeschooled students experience, since they are primarily taught at home? The first response is that homeschooling exposes students to a wide age diversity they would not have experienced in a traditional classroom. It was a regular occurrence during our co-op's weekly park dates that a diverse age range of kids came up with a game of tag or dodgeball they could all play together. No one who wanted to join was excluded. And, we could always tell when school was out as new kids showed up to the playground and we overheard, "I'm in seventh grade but you're in fifth, so I can't play with you." There is a disarming openness to homeschooled children—eager to welcome new friends no matter their age, grade, or label. As a child, I found that incredibly healing.

> Homeschooling didn't turn me into a wallflower—quite the opposite. It gave me the space to heal and grow, and to learn who I wanted to become.

The second response to the diversity question is that many homeschool families go out of their way to expose their children to perspectives and experiences outside of their own. One family in our homeschool co-op spent years studying Chinese, then arranged for their high schoolers to spend a semester volunteering with children in Taiwan (exchanging room and board for work) while strengthening their language skills. I know of other families who drive an extra distance to join co-ops from neighborhoods outside their district. It is very common for groups of homeschool families to join together for international volunteer projects, learning about another culture while working alongside locals to build improvements in the community.

In my own experience, though my parents pulled me out of school after second grade, they didn't bubble wrap me. Despite living in a small town, they made ways to expand my worldview beyond the typical summer reading list, such as inviting a homeless, pregnant teen to live in our home for four months until she got her future sorted out; inviting truckers or businessmen over for dinner to hear their stories around the table; and setting up job shadowing opportunities with professionals in the community so I could follow around a pharmacist, a biomedical engineer, and a surgeon for a day. I was even able to travel around the United States with my grandparents in their motorhome during the school year (including Las Vegas!) I was not sheltered.

What does homeschooling have to do with any of that? True, some of that "real life learning" can be recreated within a traditional school environment as well. However, being homeschooled gives students a measure of flexibility in their schedules to concentrate on topics outside the standard curriculum and consider the makings of life from a new perspective.

It also gave me the opportunity to restore some of my lost confidence from those early elementary years, so that I became fairly bold by my teens when I entered our local public high school. I was willing to stand out from the crowd, stand up for others, stand alone when necessary, and take a stand for what was I believed was right. I was named valedictorian of my class and elected student body Vice President, and went on to nationals in speech and debate. Not that my high school résumé matters a whit in my adult life, but it proves the point that homeschooling didn't turn me into a wallflower—quite the opposite. It gave me the space to heal and grow, and to learn who I wanted to become.

STATISTIC NUMBER TWO

This is the figure that I want to be especially sensitive in discussing: 17% of parents transition their child to homeschooling because they are dissatisfied with the quality of the education they are receiving.

THIS IS NOT THE PLACE WHERE I DOGPILE ONTO TEACHERS

As a former public educator, I hold teachers in high regard. Most are doing their absolute best with what they've been handed. By nature, classrooms are filled with opportunities for disruption and lost time: passing out and collecting papers, re-explaining a concept or instructions that 75% of the class got the first two times, altercations, attendance needs, and administrative interruptions. Though many teachers have creative ways to streamline classroom logistics, transitions still consume a significant amount of the day.

Add to that the sad reality that, despite rising taxes, many schools remain under-resourced and understaffed. As a teacher, even after our district approved a school levy, I still didn't have enough desks or textbooks for all my students the next fall. Even more disconcerting is the widening gap between students who come from supportive home environments and those who come to class without having eaten breakfast, who have no food in their fridge, and who lack regular adult supervision at home. In one classroom, students often have very distinct needs that one teacher must address simultaneously. Teachers are often doing their absolute best with what they've been given. So, rather than dwell further on the challenges within the system, let's talk about what is possible in a customized education.

THE CUSTOMIZED EDUCATION

At the beginning of each school year, Mom would ask me, "When do you want to be done?" I would race upstairs, chart out the number of pages, holidays, and school days, then see how many lessons I needed to complete daily to be done sometime in March. (It is an unbelievable thrill to finish school two months early; I highly recommend it.) More often than not, I would finish around my deadline and Mom would hand me the next year's math book to leisurely work through and "get ahead." With that kind of pacing, before long I was a couple grades ahead in math and loving it. She offered me the same option for the rest of my core subjects.

The library was another great resource when we were homeschooling. I still remember the first time I wandered from the children's section into the main library and discovered the shelf marked "biographies." That was the day the world of possibilities—who I could become and what it took to get there—winked at me.

For me, a customized education meant diving in headfirst, swimming as fast as I could, and sunning myself on deck as needed, the point being that I was able to push the pace of my learning based on my interests with my parents' supervision. Of course, my parents pushed me beyond my comfort zone. There was the time Mom signed me up for a course on writing essays and I thought I was going to disintegrate from the stress. (Who could possibly write five paragraphs and then let someone else read it?) Right.

For some of my homeschooled peers, a customized education meant taking classes at the local community college to supplement their high school core curriculum—all paid for by tax dollars while they earned credits they could potentially apply towards their college degrees. With the boom in online learning, students can now take courses not offered in traditional high schools, or launch themselves early into a STEM field ahead of their peers with the excess time in their school day. The possibilities stretch as far as your imagination will take you, and it doesn't necessarily require a lot of money.

One of my favorite homeschool memories was when our co-op rented out a lab at the local community college so that one of the moms, who had a master's degree in biology, could teach us anatomy. She introduced a different major animal dissection every week for a semester. Think back to when you were 11 and imagine yourself standing next to your 13-year-old friend and being handed a scalpel and a fetal pig. I was in heaven. (I almost said "hog heaven" but you might lose all respect for me.) I kept asking when we were getting our human cadavers. (Mrs. Cound thought I was joking at the time...I'm still waiting.)

I didn't realize how extraordinary that experience was until I went to high school and we spent a month building up to our first major dissection of—wait for it—an earthworm. In many ways, it wasn't until I reached my freshman year at Stanford and got to know bright students from around the world that I realized how my time learning at home had developed my taste for academic rigor, nurtured my strength of will to set high expectations for myself, and fostered a yearning for achievement not because of other's opinions but because of what I wanted for myself.

CUSTOMIZED SUPPORT

But what if it swings the other way? What if your child is struggling in a subject and needs something the school can't offer? Not surprisingly, that was the case at our house, too. On the one hand, my Mom was dealing with me (emotionally crumpled, bright, eager, quiet) and on the other hand my brother (rough and tumble, cowboy-boot-through-door-kicking strong, smart-but-hated-school). Shortly after my parents pulled me out of school, they took my brother out as well. He was almost 6 and had still not learned the basics of how to read, so his teacher said he needed to be relocated to a special-ed classroom. Had he been in need of special education assistance, my parents would have been thrilled for the help, but what he really needed was a shovel, some dirt, a bunch of rocks, and some breathing space.

So, Mom homeschooled my brother also, working diligently with him in short bursts of reading exercises broken up by long sessions of recess. The happy ending here is that he learned to read at around 8 years of age, eventually graduated from a well-known university, became a savvy businessman with a wonderful life and family, and knows how to read just fine, thanks. He just wasn't built to sit at a desk for seven hours a day as a child.

Many children aren't. Too often, a student will struggle early on in a subject—such as reading—and the negative effects of that will bleed into other subject areas. As a result, that student may begin to call herself "stupid" and be less likely to explore or push herself in case a peer sees her fail—which would make her feel even more isolated. Better, in her mind, not to try at all than to try and fail and look like a loser. As a teacher, I have seen this scenario play out too many times when students decide they can't learn before they've even given themselves the chance.

I have also seen another side of it in our homeschool communities, when students have left the traditional model where they were struggling, learned at home, recovered, and flourished. Additionally, I have seen a model where students do fine in homeschooling, but transition into a peer environment only to thrive under the positive peer pressure at school to succeed. Developing a customized education doesn't always result in homeschooling—mostly it means testing out different learning approaches in different seasons of your child's education to meet his needs.

SOMETIMES HOME IS BEST

For some students, overcoming a learning obstacle is more than mind over subject matter; some have genuine learning needs. I have two such students in my home. One in particular is high functioning and incredibly bright—you would never know Sam has a social processing disorder and a stress condition. For Sam, attending a classroom full of tapping pencils, confusing social cues, and limited body breaks would result in panic attacks. It took me five years to get Sam through Hooked on Phonics (when it took my other children less than two) because to Sam, learning was incredibly stressful.

> Simply by being the parent, you will know and love your child better than anyone else could.

Home is the best place for Sam to learn academically, not only the content but the valuable life skill of how to fail and succeed and start again. And, once schoolwork is done, we head out into the world to learn with friends through sports, groups, and classes. For Sam, the best answer was to separate academic learning from social learning in order to excel at both; as Sam matures we are providing opportunities to merge those two spheres in small ways, succeed at them, and expand from there. Being homeschooled gives Sam access to top-notch therapies and supports, where we can customize treatments into the curriculum. And, as hard as some days have been, Sam has taught me more than any of my students about time, structure, words, and flexibility. We will talk more specifically about recognizing and supporting special needs in Chapter 11.

For now, what is important to recognize is that homeschooling does not create social misfits; it makes a place for struggling students to reboot their understanding of self, retool how they learn, get the necessary supports, and learn to work and excel within their gifts.

Simply by being the parent, you will know and love your child better than anyone else could. You will get a sense of when she needs more or less of something, feels off one day and needs a break, or needs to be pushed as hard as you both can stand it to get her over the speed bump. Because you know your child best, you know how "quality" is defined, and you have the privilege of not needing to adapt that definition to 29 other students at the same time. Watching our son burn through math books, my husband looked on with jealousy one night and shook his head saying, "Man, I wish I could have learned that way." Josh was right. Everyone should be so lucky.

STATISTIC NUMBER THREE

The third reason parents choose to homeschool their kids, according to the NCES, is to incorporate faith into their educations. While historically there has been a large community of homeschoolers within the Christian faith, there are also a great many other faith families joining the community, such as Jewish, Muslim, Buddhist, and Hindu.

Schooling at home creates a unique opportunity for a child to connect with his family's religious or cultural heritage through literature, history, language, art, and music in ways he could not in a traditional school environment. And by extension, it can be a double blessing for families to explore their faith and culture together as they incorporate it into their core subjects—to continue the conversation from breakfast to dinner each day, to plan family vacations over festivals or to holy sites that are meaningful, to learn songs and traditions that represent their culture. While faith is not at all a requirement for homeschooling, if faith is important to your family, homeschooling will likely provide a meaningful way to experience it together holistically.

PRIZING INNOCENCE

Remember that national speech and debate tournament in high school I mentioned earlier? Well, believe it or not, that's where I met my husband. He was heading to Duke University as a freshman, and I was leaning into my senior year of high school, so we dated long distance with letters before the age of email. (Talk about dating myself.) Because homeschooling was such a bright spot in my childhood, it's something I talked about in our letters early on, explaining that someday I hoped to give that same gift to my children. Josh expressed concern: "I don't know about that, Anne, homeschoolers are so...weird. Present company excluded." The man had firm convictions even then and I respected that. But, beyond personal convictions, he was also teachable and willing to explore new ideas—something that made me respect him even more.

I asked him to get to know some homeschool families in his local community, which he did. He hit it off with the Hutchins family and really enjoyed their four elementary through junior high aged children. The Hutchins introduced him to two other families of homeschoolers, the Mettys and Lewises, both with four kids who became fast friends with Josh. The next thing Josh knew, he was teaching extracurricular classes once a week on philosophy and debate at the local homeschool co-op.

After a bit of time, he brought up homeschooling again. "You know, Anne, I really like those kids—the Mettys and the Lewises and the Hutchinses, their kids are so amazing."

"What's so amazing about them?" I asked.

"That they're kids," he said. "They don't care if their shoes have a brand or what cars their parents drive; they love to build forts and read books and make new friends, and they aren't intimidated by me even though I'm in college. We have great conversations—you should hear their 9-year-old talk about Tolkien! It's incredible."

Josh is right. There is something special about homeschooled kids. Innocence is a precious thing; I don't understand why our culture is so eager to help kids part with it. Innocence creates a fortress of freedom that gives children space to learn, grow, and explore unhindered. By nature, homeschooling creates a place to celebrate innocence and, as a result, extends childhood. Not that it will prevent hurt feelings; that, unfortunately, is just the way of the world. But home becomes a nurturing refuge where children can develop with freedom and safety, go out into the world to explore through activities, and then return home to distill it all into a better understanding of who they are.

IT TAKES A VILLAGE

While in some families Dad is the primary teacher, and in other families the lessons are split between parents, historically it has mostly been Mom who was the main teacher at home.

This would be a great place to pause and state the obvious: I recognize that one family can look very different from the next, and that not all homes have both Mom and Dad. One of my friends picked up homeschooling for the first time this year as a single parent, being both primary teacher and breadwinner with eager grandparents living on-site for support. I have also seen setups where both parents work—overlapping their shifts on opposite ends of the week so they can split the subjects between them—and, a variety of other creative home teaching solutions with tutors and neighbors and aunties in the mix.

While I recognize and celebrate that there are a lot of unique ways to learn at home, my anecdotes about my being the primary teacher and my husband the principal may not speak to your family's roles. And that's the beauty of homeschooling—customization. To those families with a teaching arrangement that looks different from mine, thank you for reading along with patience and modifying pronouns as needed—the advice and tools in this book will be helpful for all families, no matter who is teaching.

That disclaimer made, however your family chooses to structure teaching roles, I encourage you to find someone in your community who can act as an outlet and support for you. Someone you can reach out to as needed in whatever combination of frustration, celebration, confusion, elation, or tears you might be experiencing. Someone who can provide encouragement, back you up to your students, or give tangible help at the end of the day. It may be a spouse, a relative, or a friend. It could be a handful of friends—it takes a village. And, if it takes a little while to assemble your village, that's OK—just keep it on your radar and continue to work toward building it.

> Find someone in your community who can act as an outlet and support for you.

In fact, one of the reasons families choose to homeschool is *because* it takes a village. For many, there is something special about the community collaboration of doing life together, where academics merge with home and lifestyle to create a holistic approach to learning.

ARE ALL THESE YOURS?

When well-intended strangers approach me in the grocery expressing concern about the social wellbeing of the row of children trailing behind me well within school hours, I'm happy to answer.

There are so many ways I could express how thankful I am to be able to give my children a chance to learn independently—to have a curriculum customized to pushing ahead in their strengths rather than waiting for the class to catch up; to support them in the areas where they need it most without them feeling lesser for it; to remove social challenges from the equation so they can do school with parents and then play with friends afterwards, succeeding better at both;

to discover and grow in a subject area that may not be available in a traditional school; to spend the best parts of their childhood on concentrated learning and a variety of activities; to love learning for themselves.

I see these strangers' questions as an opportunity to invite them to join me at our kitchen table, and I am grateful.

[1] A fascinating dissertation on "Centuries of Tutoring: A Perspective of Childhood Education" by Edward Gordon, Loyola University Chicago, 1988. https://ecommons.luc.edu/cgi/viewcontent.cgi?article=3558&context=luc_diss

[2] National Center for Education Statistics. https://nces.ed.gov/programs/schoolchoice/ind_05.asp

2

Is Homeschooling Right for Me?

Assessing the Need

Homeschooling isn't for everyone. I grew up swimming competitively and yet I am paying someone to coach my children how to swim. Just because we know how to do something as parents doesn't mean we need to be solely responsible for teaching it to our kids, even if we can do it well. I don't love my children less because I hired a coach to teach them the butterfly; neither do I love them more because I am homeschooling them versus enrolling them in our neighborhood school.

That being said, almost anyone is capable of homeschooling.

Parents curious about teaching their children at home often ask, "What does a good home education look like? When should I delegate some of that instruction to outside co-ops, tutors, the district, or online courses? And how do I know if it's working?"

These are thoughtful questions I have entertained from parents countless times over the years. All homeschooling parents at some point worry that they aren't doing enough—the responsibility of education, social formation, and extracurricular development rests heavily on their shoulders, and for good reason. Preparing a child for life as a fully functioning adult is a significant role. But chances are, if parents are asking any of the above questions and finding resources such as *Homeschool Like an Expert*, they are on the right track.

WHEN IT DOESN'T WORK

A majority of this chapter will be devoted to answering the titular question and walking through how to make homeschooling work. But rather than start with sunshine and rainbows, let's get real and start with sunburn and puddles: when homeschooling doesn't work.

A very close friend of mine (we'll call her Sandy) was strongly encouraged by her husband to homeschool their children. A bright woman with charisma, strength, and a passion for her kids, she was not neutral on this subject—she honestly did not want to homeschool them. She envisioned butting heads with her willful 9-year-old son and being unable to provide enough stimulation for her creative 7-year-old daughter. "How is this even possible?" she lamented to me on the phone.

We talked through all the factors to consider around finances, support, and the needs of everyone involved. I tried to let her off the hook with the same advice I shared above: "Homeschooling your children is not proof that you love them." She agreed. But she was eager to hear her husband's side of things and, despite her misgivings, assured me she really was willing to give it a try.

> All homeschooling parents at some point worry that they aren't doing enough.

"But what if I fail?" she asked. "Failing is not discovering that homeschooling doesn't work for you; failure is being so afraid of it not working that you never try," I replied. (Admittedly, I thought Yoda would be proud.)

We talked about some initial structures she could put into place, with a local homeschool support group at the top of the list. She was able to find one, and they welcomed her eagerly and provided all kinds of support.

By the end of the school year, Sandy called to tell me she had learned a lot. She had learned about her kids, discovered more about how each learns best, and had some great times together as a family. However, in the end, Sandy and her husband decided the cost to the family in time and finances was greater than the tradeoffs. Sandy had decided to go back to work around the same time she found out they were expecting, so she and James agreed it was best for the older two kids to go back to school.

And they did.

And they were just fine.

They were no worse for the wear after their year of homeschooling, and Sandy told me later she was so glad she had given it a go. "Not everyone is meant to teach their kids at home," she told me, "and after homeschooling them for a year I have an even better idea about how to support their teachers and be proactive on the home front in their education. As experiments go, it was a win." I agreed.

So while this is a true story of when homeschooling *doesn't* work, it is also a story of when it *does*. That year of time together gave Sandy a deeper perspective on and appreciation of her children's education, and strengthened the teamwork between her and her husband as they pressed forward into helping their kids learn from others. Academically, their kids continued on seamlessly. Count that as a win.

WHAT TO CONSIDER

Before running out to purchase curriculum, here are a few points to consider. (And, if you are partnering with your spouse to educate your children, it will be especially important to work through these questions together so you can align yourselves on goals and expectations.)

QUALIFICATIONS

First, check your state's requirements to make sure you can homeschool legally. (For a quick resource to locate your state's requirements, visit Links to Experts on HomeschoolExpert.com. We'll discuss the legal side of homeschooling in depth in Chapter 5.)

Teaching your children at home does not require a teaching degree, but often it does require some sort of high school-level diploma or education. Among the inspirational books I have read about parents pushing their children beyond the educational norm is Ben Carson's autobiography, *Gifted Hands*. (Spoiler alert: He goes from poverty-stricken inner-city kid in Detroit in a single-parent household to one of the world's most prominent pediatric neurosurgeons.)

Whether or not you agree with his politics, his life story is impressive. Dr. Carson credits his mom with making that possible. Sonya, who dropped out of school in the third grade, was married at age 13, soon left by her husband with two small boys, and struggled to make ends meet though she worked two or even three jobs. After watching her boys settle to the bottom of the class year after year, Sonya decided one day to limit their TV time and enforce strict rules around completing homework before play, going so far as to assign them the additional work of reading two library books a week and turning in to her weekly written reports. Reports, Carson later realized, his mom could barely read.

Their grades rose dramatically. What inspires me most about Sonya is that she didn't need impressive qualifications to supplement her sons' education at home and compel them to academic excellence; she needed high expectations and the strength to push them toward something greater. Personal grit is often worth more in homeschooling than a Ph.D.

Variations on Homeschooling

There are four categories of schooling: Public, Private, Public Homeschool, and Private Homeschool—each are available online, in person, or some combination of the two.

How you choose to homeschool your child will impact your flexibility, your financial cost, and your freedom of choice.

Traditionally there have been three categories for schooling at home. Thanks to COVID-19, now there are four. When schooling at home during COVID-19 began, the media was abuzz with suggestions—mostly well-intended but from people who have never schooled at home—about how to homeschool on the fly. Homeschooling is very different from traditional education and as a result many of the suggestions were not helpful for parents schooling students from home.

Please note the infographic to see how the difference matters. On the left there are four education categories: Public, Private, Public Homeschool, and Private Homeschool. Above them are two versions for each category: Online and Offline. You can see that, because of COVID-19, all four categories of education are now offered at home either online or offline. The terms for these categories can vary by state, but the general descriptions apply.

The key factors to consider across these four types of schooling are cost, autonomy, and authority. By these I mean the financial cost families must pay outside the traditional classroom for online memberships or curriculum; the autonomy to decide how, when, where, and what to study; and the authority to determine assessment, teacher requirements, and timing of the school year.

PUBLIC SCHOOL: ONLINE

Starting top left is Public Online School, which was part of the traditional school district long before COVID-19. These courses were *designed* to be offered online through the district as a part of its approved course load using prerecorded lessons, interactive digital reading material, and online exams.

These online courses are still available within many districts but, like other classes, typically must be enrolled in prior to the beginning of a semester. They are also fully under the authority of the school district as part of the official public school curriculum. The key differences to point out about Public Online School is that parents are not responsible for the cost, nor do they have the authority to choose the brand of curriculum, day of study, or format — that authority belongs fully to the school. So cost is low, autonomy is low, authority is low.

4 Ways to Educate at Home

	ONLINE			OFFLINE		
Public	L	L	L	L	L	L
Private	M/H	S	L	M/H	S	L
Public Homeschool	S	S	L	S	S	L
Private Homeschool	M/H	H	H	M/H	H	H

■ Cost
■ Autonomy
■ Authority

S Shared
L Low
M Moderate
H High

PUBLIC SCHOOL: OFFLINE

Offline public school is "emergency public school at home," also called Zoom-schooling, and is what families enrolled in public school experienced at the beginning of the COVID crisis. Offline public school is regulated, evaluated, and funded by the state. Even though it occurs within a student's home, by definition offline public school is *not* homeschooling because the district is still in charge of when and how schooling is administered. It is a temporary solution to an emergency situation, and some families found it to be a good fit.

As a former public educator, I have a significant amount of respect for the thousands of teachers who adapted lesson plans online overnight to reach their students during this difficult period. Any challenges I bring up about Zoomschool are not a reflection of the quality of our teachers, but of these difficult times. Similar to Public Online School, cost is low, autonomy is low, authority is low.

PRIVATE SCHOOL: ONLINE

There are many private online schools that have been a very helpful resource to parents during the COVID-19 crisis. Developed with online study, assessment, and engagement in mind, these programs are often high quality. By enrolling in a private online school, cost is moderate to high, accountability is shared, and autonomy is low.

PRIVATE SCHOOL: OFFLINE

Similar to traditional public schools, private schools developed their own online strategy during COVID-19, where work typically done in the classroom setting was transferred online. For this, cost is moderate to high, accountability is shared, autonomy is low.

PUBLIC HOMESCHOOLING

Public Homeschooling is a hybrid between public school and private homeschooling, often called "charter schools" or "public school at home" depending on your state. Parents who choose to homeschool through a charter are reimbursed by the state to cover a specific list of curricular and extracurricular expenses, often $1,000 or more per student per year.

Along with those funds come support and accountability from the state, requiring parents to meet with a Teacher of Record every few weeks to design lesson plans and show proof of work. For parents new to homeschooling or wanting more accountability, this can be a beneficial arrangement, offering some autonomy over content as well as support from the district. And within the category of Public Homeschooling, parents can select online, offline, or a fusion of the two.

It's worth noting that Public Homeschooling comes with strings attached, as it should—it is a slightly more malleable form of public school because it is located in the student's home, is directed by the parent and district, and is partially funded by the state. So cost is shared, autonomy is shared, authority is low.

PRIVATE HOMESCHOOLING

Private Homeschooling is the most customizable of all the forms of schooling, and is the traditional form of homeschooling that sought legalization in the 1980s. Parents who choose this model do so because they want to tailor the pace, curriculum, schedule, and focus of their child's education.

This form of schooling provides families with the greatest amount of autonomy, empowering them to customize their curriculum and school schedule to fit their needs. Similar to Public Homeschooling, parents can select online, offline, or a fusion of the two. That means cost is moderate to high, autonomy is high, and authority is high.

TAKE YOUR PICK

Which of the four modes best fits your family is up to you. Your family is not my family; your method of schooling may not be my method of schooling. Consider the tradeoffs of cost, autonomy, and authority, and ask yourself: "What is the best way to prioritize them given my family's needs? What about my child's needs? Are there creative ways to make this possible with my work schedule?"

Parents in the U.S. retain the legal right over their child to disenroll from or re-enroll in public school at many points in the year if they meet their state's criteria, even in the face of COVID-19. Every state has different requirements, so check out links on HomeschoolExpert.com to discover yours.

I will also add that homeschooling is a lot like a wedding—it costs as much money as you have to spend. I have seen parents provide an excellent education by purchasing beautiful high-end curriculum, hire private tutors, and send their children on international learning tours. I have also seen parents provide an excellent education with a modest budget, handing their students a math book, a library card, a reading list, and internet access.

Among other things, 2020 will likely be remembered for giving families a new perspective on education—that school can be something new, that there is more than one way to learn, and that home might be a great place to have school after all.

CAREER FLEXIBILITY

Parents often cite homeschooling's flexibility and adaptability as key benefits. Keeping that in mind, there is nothing magical about having school on a weekday morning between September and May.

Think outside the box for a moment: What would it look like to homeschool over the weekend for half the day and then finish up schoolwork together on weekday evenings, or whenever you are off work? What would it look like for one parent to teach math and science and the other to teach history, literature, and writing—and by combining them in that way doing less work by tackling multiple subjects at once? What would it look like to cover fewer hours of school work each week over 12 months a year instead of schooling for more hours each week over nine months? At the end of the year, the time of day or day of the week is irrelevant as long as your student has mastered the material.

I have known dual-income households where parents space out shifts and divide subject areas between each to cover during the week. I have known single moms who teach their children the core content on the weekend, leave them with online assignments to do with Nana while Mom goes to work, and Mom comes home in the evening to check the work and answer any questions. I have also known neighborhoods where each household hosts Podschool for one day a week, and the neighborhood kids rotate between houses in a One Schoolhouse Model.

With a ratio of 1:1 or even 1:4, it takes two to four hours a day to school an elementary student, four to six hours to school a junior higher, and five to seven hours to school a high school student at home—and that's with no extra homework.

As long as we're on the subject of homework, many parents I talk to assume that homeschooling is the same as doing homework all day—but there are three key differences. First, parents who coach their students on homework in the evening may not know the context for the lesson or the teacher's expectations. Second, they are likely working with a student who is weary from having been in school all day. And third, they have to drill their students through completing all the work whether or not the student understands the concept.

That sounds a lot harder to me than homeschooling, where I customize the lesson to my student's needs, we get it done when my student is fresh, and he leaves the table feeling accomplished and ready to embrace the rest of the day. Both methods involve books and a kitchen table, but the process, autonomy, and flexibility are completely different.

BUDGET

A good place to start in assessing whether or not homeschooling is a fit for your family is the cost. The average private homeschooling family spends about $800 per student per year on education-related costs,[1] with that number potentially decreasing for families with multiple children who are able to share costs, sometimes as low as $400 per student.

It is an incredibly valuable exercise to build a homeschool budget, including fees for co-ops or extra homeschool classes along with curriculum. In that budget also estimate money you will save by serving the kids leftovers for lunch, spending less on fads your kids may want for school, and reducing cell phone plans for kids if they have them (since they are home, they can just use wi-fi). It's also worth looking at places you can make your own tradeoffs. What conveniences would you be willing to give up so you could pad your budget in other areas?

For me, one of the biggest perks of having been homeschooled was taking family vacations while other kids were in school. Every second week of September my parents would drive down the West Coast, staying with family along the way, until we got to the beaches of Southern California—beaches that were empty of tourists but just as beautiful as they were the week before school started. We even got to go to Disneyland one year with my grandparents, waiting in line for a whole five minutes at the newly opened Splash Mountain because everyone else was at school. Pretty glorious. As an adult, I now realize that my parents were able to make all that fit in the budget because off-peak rates were more affordable. Dream big.

STUDENT NEEDS

Sometimes the driving impetus for homeschooling is that the student needs a change—for social, academic, physical, or life circumstances. As was true in my own story, parents sometimes feel pushed into homeschooling whether or not it is their personal ambition because that is what seems best for their children in that season. If that is you, take comfort in knowing you are not alone. Many parents share that same story of homeschooling because that's what their children needed. There are resources available to help parents equip themselves quickly for the task; *Homeschool Like an Expert: Video Series* is a great start.

FAMILY GOALS

There are three different ways to think about developing family homeschool goals—and if you already feel like your head is going to explode with new content, feel free to pause after the first one and put a pin in the other two to circle back to later in the year.

First, start with the bottom up, thinking about tangible goals for this year. These are often the easiest goals to envision because they are the most obvious to you already about your child. For example, do you want your child this year to transition to chapter books or learn to tie her shoes; do you want your son to develop follow-through, memorize the multiplication tables, or learn to drive the car? Simply knowing your child as you do, you can look for reasonable areas of growth holistically this year that you want her to develop. Academic goals are largely driven by your curriculum and state standards, so we will cover that more in Chapters 8 and 10.

You have already taken a big step by deciding to homeschool, so if that feels like plenty of goal setting for right now, this is where you put that pin. Keep reading though, since it helps to be mindful of these other two goal areas as you go through your first year so that your direction will become clearer as you spend more concentrated time with your children and get to know other homeschool families.

The second goal area is core family values. Ask yourself these questions: "What does our family believe is at the center of who we are and why we do what we do? Are there principles or beliefs we share that could resonate through our learning lifestyle? How do I want my children to view me as their teacher parent, and how does that affect how I teach them?"

As you set and aim for goals, be patient with your student and especially yourself.

The third goal area is the top down, which are the end game goals. Ask yourself these questions: "What kind of person do I want my child to be when he is 18 in terms of his character, abilities, independence, and adaptability? What do I want to remember most from our homeschooling journey together?" Try to think of what you want at the end and then work backward to what you must practically do this year. Some people have an easier time setting goals bottom up, others top down—use whatever order makes the most sense to you. I revisit our goals *throughout* the year *every* year because it provides both validation and direction to my days.

As you build these three categories of goals, be sure to include reachable goals along with stretch goals. Very little good happens without planning. At the end of each quarter, reflect back on how your goals are working and where you need to recalibrate, adjust, or flex. Sometimes it is a good reminder partway through the year that you were hoping to do more science experiments with the kids than you actually have, and written goals can help steer you back on course. At the end of the year you will know what was too much, not enough, or just right; all that input will go into helping you plan for the next year.

Finally, as you set and aim for goals, be patient with your student and especially yourself. I know—I just encouraged you to build stretch goals into your plan, but if this is your first year of homeschooling please don't make it too hard in the beginning. It's better to have some early wins and build momentum than to set unrealistic goals that leave you burned out and frustrated before the end of the year.

Homeschooling is kitchen-table-friendly, so don't feel like you need to create a special schoolroom in your home—you may not end up using it anyway. Remember, homeschooling is radically different from traditional schooling. Those of us who used to play teacher as kids stood before an imaginary row of desks and a chalkboard and lectured. (Or, maybe that was just me.) But learning at home is not a lecture—it is a conversation between you and your child.

Working together at the table will help maintain accountability with your kids, as well as make it easier for you to multitask between students if you have more than one child.

While you don't need a dedicated classroom at home, you do need a storage area for easy access to school boxes, like a kitchen cabinet or hall closet. In our family, each child has their own student box filled with a scratch notebook, journal, current textbooks, current independent reading, and a container of supplies. Similarly, my teacher box is filled with answer keys, a planner, student folders for completed work, a folder of different kinds of paper, and my container of supplies. We try to be disciplined about keeping school supplies in our school boxes to help streamline our morning and get work done efficiently. Of course, there have been seasons of life when we have needed to take schoolwork on the road, so I created a secondary To Go Box so that, again, everything is where we need it to be and there is no excuse for not getting work done.

As tempting as it is to let your kids complete geography worksheets in their treehouse or study literature in their pajamas, lean away from it. Flexible structure is your friend (we will get super practical about that in Chapter 7), and making it part of your daily routine will definitely help you work at a healthy pace. So discuss together where you can make a dedicated workspace and what that might look like.

Our family has school at the kitchen table daily, and I stash our school charts inside cabinet doors so that at the end of the day our kitchen still looks like a kitchen (which helps me turn off my teacher brain at the end of the day). That's what works for our family, and I have seen incredibly diverse variations for others, all the way up to a kitchen that looks like they cook in a classroom. It's up to your family to discover what works best for you.

MANAGING EXPECTATIONS

There seems to be an inverse relationship to the number of years spent homeschooling and the amount of needs parents are willing to outsource. In other words, the longer families homeschool, the more they seem to expect that they must do and be everything for their child. This is unrealistic. Just as in my swimming example at the beginning of this chapter, sometimes it is not only necessary but valuable to invite others into a teaching relationship with your child.

Sometime around when my eldest was in fifth grade, we were discussing that he had three years left of homeschooling and then he was off to high school. "What? You mean you aren't going to homeschool me through college?!?" Sweet boy, no. Much as he thought at the time he would have liked it, he will have many teachers and coaches in his life beyond me, and teaching our homeschooled children how to learn from others is a life skill.

The question then becomes, "When is the right time to delegate that role?" Some examples are easy: We wanted our children to learn Chinese from a young age and didn't speak the language ourselves, so we hired a babysitter to speak it to them when she was at our house. Other examples are not so straightforward: If my son is struggling with grammar and parts of speech year after year, how do I pinpoint if the problem is the curriculum, the student, or the teacher (or some combination)—and decide that a tutor would be helpful?

Sometimes there are subjects that you are more than capable of teaching (such as essay writing), but the opportunity to work with peers in a workshop format and to read finished work aloud together might be of more benefit through a co-op than if you were to teach it at home. Or not. Ultimately it comes down to this: What does your budget allow, what does your child need for basic subject coverage, what is a "nice to have" addition to your curriculum, and when is too much no longer a good thing and you need to scale back? These are all questions to consider as you look to meet your student's needs. Just don't feel like you have to be their everything—support systems are there for a reason.

OFF TO A ROUGH START?

For some families, such as my parents, homeschooling becomes an option when school turns sour and learning is overwhelmed by classroom stressors. In this instance, I would strongly encourage parents to begin homeschooling slowly.

The reason for this is simple: Education has unfortunately become negatively linked in your child's mind to the troubling or hurtful experiences he felt in the classroom. It will be important in the early weeks to give him space to recover and lead off with some gentle guidelines more around home management than academics. Consider providing him with a warmup schedule for when to start the day, eat meals, finish chores, and read—this goes for elementary and a variation even into high school. Sometimes, a recovery period is needed. Children who have experienced bullying or trauma need time to detox from negative learning patterns or self-perceptions—how much time they need will depend on how much hurt they have experienced and for how long.

Kids absorb misconceptions about their value and identity from peers so easily when they are young that sometimes negative self-perceptions could take a year or even more to work out. That's not to say you should abandon school for a year, but be flexible about how you transition back into it.

This may be the only place in this book where you hear me say this, so enjoy it while you can: Set lower expectations your first year if your student is transitioning out of a dysfunctional school situation. Give him time to heal, recover, establish a new healthy rhythm of learning at home, and discover that learning isn't stressful but can be fun.

> Sometimes it is not only necessary but valuable to invite others into a teaching relationship with your child.

Once you have moved past the initial warmup schedule, begin to layer in one new core subject every week or two until you have all five subjects in the rotation (math, reading, writing, science, history) and then pause at that level for a few months. If your student is in high school, you can layer up to seven core subjects. The bottom line is to give them time to get their bearings and feel successful with their core subjects before adding extracurricular subjects or time constraints into their routine.

In addition to slowly ramping up the curriculum, make time to set goals. Sometimes just getting your student showered, dressed, and finished with breakfast by 9:00AM may seem Olympic—if so, start with that. For other kids, getting them to read one book a week is stretching it—start there.

But work out a reasonable, measurable goal or two in the beginning so he (and you!) can see his progress and celebrate meeting it together. As with my daughter who needed five years and piles of patience to learn how to read, now that she's got it figured out she is a voracious reader. Giving your child a chance to recover, find his new pace, and gain a confident footing in the new normal will pay off later if you don't push too hard in the beginning.

BUT WHAT IF I RUIN MY CHILD?

Nearly all parents have seasons of worry that we are not providing enough for our children. It is a natural result of the constant self-evaluation that comes with being a homeschooler combined with the parent guilt that is delivered free of charge alongside our children. Because their education, social formation, and extracurricular interests sit squarely on our shoulders, it *should* require extra focus on our part.

The parents that raise my concern, actually, are those who are perpetually unconcerned. If you approach the role of parent teacher with humility and intentionality, you are probably going to do just fine. Anticipate that you will constantly be adapting and retooling to meet your child's needs from year to year, and that what worked for one child will most likely not work the same way for a sibling. Flexibility is the name of the game, and recalibrating and adjusting is a big part of your job.

Our children are like trees in an orchard. When they begin to sprout as saplings, we really have very little idea what kind of fruit they will bear or what resources they will need to reach their full potential. It is only as our little trees grow into bigger trees that we begin to understand their needs more fully, and as a result adapt support systems, nourishment, and shelter or exposure to meet those needs. How I support the branches for one sapling will not look the same as how I stake out the trunk for another. If you are not a gardener and this metaphor leaves you behind, think of it this way—it is the gardener's responsibility to provide what the tree needs as much as is humanly possible; beyond that, it is up to the tree to grow.

Your investment in your child's education at home will not only *not* ruin her, it will foster wonderful memories as a family. When I was growing up, my parents had great relationships with my brothers and me, and we still do. I am grateful to them for fostering my love for learning and creativity in our home.

---

[1] How much parents should spend on homeschooling is similar to the question of how much couples should spend on a wedding—the answer is, you can always spend more. Sources vary, but $800 per student per year seems to be a safe bet. https://www.time4learning.com/blog/new-homeschooler/how-much-does-homeschooling-cost/

3

What About Social Needs?

Learning With Friends

O ne of the first questions everyone asks about homeschooling is, "What about social needs?". Given how homeschooling may have been perceived up until recently, this is an important question to ask—and an encouraging one to answer.

HOW SOCIAL GROWTH MATTERS

Nearly everyone can agree *that* the social aspect of learning matters. So rather than reinforcing a point we already support, let's look at *how* social matters to education. Many readers begin from the vantage point that combining social experiences with academics is desirable, so let's evaluate that assumption by peeling the two apart.

What would it look like to divide a school day, with one half devoted to study and the other half to opportunities with friends? For a wide spectrum of students this can be beneficial, because separating studies from play can accomplish two things.

First, for the homeschooler, there are academic benefits: Some students are able to engage with the content in a more focused way without distraction, pursue it at their own pace, and learn without concerns about standing out from their peers. The ratio of teacher to student at home makes learning highly supportive and adaptive. Certainly, traditional schooling provides opportunities for group projects, class presentations, and collaboration, but none of that is limited to traditional school. Homeschooling parents can select extracurricular activities that specifically address those needs

Second, outside of that concentrated home learning space, the student is then able to fully engage with peers in sports, co-ops, play dates, and activity clubs that are more conducive to collaboration and socialization. Instead of discouraging students from interacting during classwork, we are encouraging interaction because work is done. So, it is not a question of *if* homeschoolers engage with peers, but *when* and *how*.

Beyond that is the benefit of exposure to diversity. Homeschoolers are often lauded for their ability to engage in conversation with adults and children of all ages, because that is what they are used to doing every day. Rather than match students to classmates largely on the merits of being born within six to 12 months of each other, it is far more successful to learn practical communication and collaboration strategies by working and playing with people from diverse age groups and backgrounds.

This is especially true if the content a student is learning is a better fit given his intelligence, ability, and maturity instead of a grade level based on birth year. Homeschooling creates an organic space to develop a lifestyle of learning within our community, engaging with content and people at a variety of levels.

At this point, it is worth pausing for a moment to ask ourselves why we value the social element being paired with academics, and what is the best way to meet those needs for each student. Further, are we thinking too narrowly about what we mean by "social"? Developing a socially skilled child involves more than interaction with peers—it refers to thriving with a broad set of life skills applied to learning environments as well as the outside world. All kids need to be social. All kids need academics. But they don't necessarily need to be combined simultaneously to build a healthy student into a capable, relatable adult.

I DON'T WANT MY KID TO BE WEIRD

While the term "weird" to describe any child is understandably offensive and hurtful, it is especially demeaning to families of children with special needs who have worked incredibly hard to succeed at basic tasks—like putting on shoes without a 30-minute panic attack that it might be the wrong foot, or learning how to respond with words instead of fists.

I have lived that life; I understand.

Nonetheless, "weird" is the label often ringing in the ears of the community, as well as "awkward," "isolated," or "deprived" when discussing homeschoolers. In order to better understand why those adjectives became so closely linked with homeschooling—as opposed to more positive, accurate perspectives around the benefits of a customized education model—let's go back to the 1980s.

When homeschooling first became legal in the state where I lived, many of the families choosing to teach their children at home did so because the traditional public school system could not meet the needs of their kids. As I came to learn in the course of my own university certification in education, this was largely due to school systems in that era being relatively new in understanding how to support students with unique learning needs, such as dyslexia, ADHD, Autism, Asperger's, and various social processing disorders. Some of the necessary support systems had not yet been developed in schools, as the diagnoses themselves were somewhat new and unfamiliar. As a result, many families chose to teach their special-needs kids at home.

While not all the students being homeschooled in this early era required special support systems and therapies, that is what got the most press. As a result, "socially challenged" and "homeschooled" became initially and inaccurately linked.

Just as it is offensive to call a special-needs child "awkward," it is equally hurtful to many homeschoolers when they are questioned about their child being "socially deprived." To be fair, sometimes the question is simply a sign of ignorance on the part of the person asking. Nonetheless, I have seen many homeschoolers graciously respond to this query over the years.

How we meet social needs outside of the classroom must be addressed intentionally. Parents teaching their children at home through a variety of methods is in a significant season of expansion. With an entire generation of former homeschooled students having grown up to lead healthy, bright, productive, culturally relevant adult lives (and many millions of families launching into homeschooling currently) I suspect at some point the social question will diminish.

> Homeschooling creates an organic space to develop a lifestyle of learning within our community, engaging with content and people at a variety of levels.

Eventually, the social adaptability of homeschoolers will be normalized across the population. In the meantime, I encourage homeschooling families to continue to advocate graciously about how we meet our children's holistic needs whenever asked.

SOCIAL IMPLICATIONS IN TRADITIONAL SCHOOLS

Oftentimes, when I am approached by people in the community asking about social needs, I will start by asking them their views. Namely, what do they think of the impact of the social factor on students within the classroom? Some think social interaction is a good idea, others might reference bullying or peer pressure, but overall the idea of doing school with friends links the two concepts so that they are difficult to initially separate in the conversation.

So, depending on how much time we have, I might tell them about a few of my former students, for whom the social element made learning harder. I first think of Stan, a boy with thick glasses who sat at the front of my class just so he could see the board. He was eager to learn, but was regularly pushed around by his peers for being a "nerd"; eventually, he gave up asking questions in class so they would leave him alone.

> After homeschooling for a year you can always enroll your child in school if it isn't a good fit —no harm done.

Then I think about Leena, a sophomore who discovered she was pregnant and decided she would place the baby for adoption, but soon dropped out of school as a result of her classmates regularly criticizing and deriding her for choosing adoption. The only solution she knew of was to leave campus permanently.

Then there was Kira, a smart young woman who was eager to excel but became discouraged even in her honors classes when she was regularly held back from pressing deeper into the content because her peers could not keep up.

Of all my students, the one who stands out to me the most is Joe. I came to learn after the fact that Joe had been slow to read and as a result was mislabeled in elementary school. As he aged through the system, teachers going forward read his file and expected less of him; he became violent. I didn't know any of this about him when he entered my class the first day.

Like my other students, I told Joe he had a clean slate with me and I wanted his best. One day the school counselor came to my class to accuse me of padding Joe's grade. If I'm honest, Joe really wasn't even on my radar at that point. He was a solid B student. When I pulled up his work samples and showed his progress in class, the counselor let down his guard and explained that Joe was failing every other class and had recently thrown a desk through a classroom window. Joe? Really? We both left that conversation a little stunned by Joe's potential.

All of these were my true students, anonymized of course. In each case—teaching them in a class with 29 peers and knowing what I did about a customized education—I desperately wished I could have homeschooled them all.

This is usually the turning point in the conversation. I don't think a lot of people in the community question the value or efficacy of putting 30 kids in a room together to learn a subject, asking what impact the quantity of bodies has on the quality of learning. And yet, on the whole, the community is consistently concerned with whether homeschooled kids are interacting socially with other kids as part of their formation. There is so much more to consider in developing a holistically healthy student.

For many students, the trade-offs of learning in a traditional school will outweigh any challenges that might occur learning alongside peers—and that is great. As I said at the beginning of the book, there are many ways to get an education—homeschooling is just one of them. The real question is, which way is best for your student.

SOCIAL IMPLICATIONS IN HOMESCHOOL

Assuming the people who asked me about the social element of homeschooling are still standing there, we might start to discuss what an ideal education could look like. What would it mean for a student to progress at the speed he needed? What would it mean for a student to engage in the subject matter in a way that was customized to her learning style? What would it mean for a group of students to cluster together organically for field trips, park days, and extracurriculars based on interests rather than an age or grade, learning to converse or collaborate with their peers at all levels.

A friend told me once that homeschoolers have an "aroma"—he quickly clarified that he wasn't talking about hygiene, but more a wholesome, unbroken spark of curiosity that was evident. And he was right.

There is something special about having conversations with my children's homeschooled friends—they are often eager to be heard, ask questions, and tell me about their day. Similarly, they don't feel discouraged from befriending someone because their grade levels are different. And I have never heard one homeschooler ridicule another for being a nerd—smartness is consistently a hallmark. If anything, friends are proud of each other when they discover someone is especially bright at a subject. If anything, the friend might lament that the subject doesn't come as easily to him.

Growing up, when our family would go on field trips or outings, it was one of my mom's favorite things to temporarily disguise the fact we were homeschooled. In the course of our day, we would talk with adults and play with children of all ages. Whether we were off on an adventure or in line at the grocery store, perfect strangers would remark to my mom with wonder about how we were "respectful," "polite," "interesting," or "open." Mom would thank them, and when they were finished, she would add like a cherry on top, "they're homeschooled," and wait for the stunned look to momentarily freeze the person's face. Homeschoolers were still a bit like space aliens when I was a child—everyone had heard about them, but it was unclear if any had been spotted. Time and again, the stranger's delighted surprise was the best part. And, most importantly, we weren't putting on an act—we were too young to be anyone but ourselves. Who they saw was genuinely who we were.

A PRIVILEGE TO ANSWER

By this point, my new friends and I have likely ended our conversation about the social implications of homeschooling, hopefully with me having answered their questions graciously, honestly, and insightfully to help them consider alternative education from a new perspective. It is not my job to convince anyone to love homeschooling. But I consider it a privilege to answer their questions.

For the parent considering becoming the sole educator at home, this decision feels like a big step. Sometimes, outside criticism can make that simple step feel life-altering. First, I would encourage you to remind yourself that after homeschooling for a year you can always enroll your child in school if it isn't a good fit (like Sandy in Chapter 2) —no harm done. Choosing to homeschool your child does not have to be a "forever and ever" kind of decision.

Second, I would remind you that opinions are typically worth what you pay for them. Certainly, hear people's questions and concerns for what they are— then, seek out wise counsel from teachers and experienced homeschool parents. After sifting through the advice, keep the gold and ignore the rubble. Even when it is well intended by people you love.

Instead, use specific goals and standards instead of fear and guilt to gauge your success (more on how to measure that in the coming chapters) and remind yourself that nothing worth doing comes easily or quickly. Chapter 4 will look thoughtfully at how to build a strong social network for your homeschooled child, so keep reading for next steps on this subject.

Like most everything else, educating well (and seeing the fruit of those efforts) takes time and is worth waiting for.

4

How Do I Find Other Homeschoolers?

Building a Community

At first blush, homeschooling seems like an isolating adventure—images of a solitary Conestoga wagon and *Little House on the Prairie* probably lurk in the periphery of your memory. Fortunately, it is anything but that. In the last 30 years the number of families educating their children at home has grown exponentially, with local groups and the internet providing a dense network of support, resources, friendship, and comradery. If anything, the trouble is not finding a homeschool group to join, it is restraining yourself from joining too many.

WHY DO I NEED COMMUNITY?

Becoming a part of a local homeschool community has been critical both to my success as a parent teacher and to the overall education of my children. At times, homeschooling can be isolating—not as much for my children as it is for me.

Many days I spend the bulk of my time as teacher, mentor, disciplinarian, chef, or chauffeur, and that can lead to loneliness, a limited perspective, or burnout if I am not intentional to build social outlets into my week. The kids are doing great—they are the ones getting driven to sports and playdates; I'm the one still in the car. Developing a healthy connection with other families will give you not only a sense of belonging, but access to resources that will help you homeschool confidently.

It will also give you a place to brainstorm with other parents who understand your world and what it means to homeschool. Envision a day when your child is struggling with handwriting (again!) and you head to the park to meet up with six other homeschool families that afternoon. While there, you have the opportunity to vent, strategize, and query other parents who have likely experienced similar struggles—which is not only therapeutic, it often leads to discovering new helpful resources. In my early years of homeschooling, I walked away from many of those kinds of conversations feeling heard, helped, and grateful to be a part of something larger than myself.

Furthermore, a homeschool community is a source of validation—and not just for what you experience as a parent teacher. It is immensely helpful for our children to see their peers with other teaching parents because it reinforces for them our lifestyle of learning, our purpose, and our unique roles. We have discovered so much from observing how other homeschool families study similarly or differently from ours, and it has challenged my children in positive ways to see their peers creatively stretch themselves.

Perhaps the greatest benefit from being a part of one of these groups is the opportunity to learn from experienced homeschooling parents within your community. Most are eager to share resources, ideas, lessons learned the hard way, and helps. *Homeschool Like an Expert* (both this book and its companion video series) is my way of distilling decades of park day conversations into tangible resources that will help you homeschool confidently, just as so many expert homeschoolers helped me.

WHERE ARE THE HOMESCHOOLERS?

Depending on your community involvement with scouts, service, or sports, it may be relatively easy to locate a homeschool family. All you really need is one person who can connect you to others.

As you already know, it's great to start your search online—not just searching keywords but also specifically seeking groups on social media platforms. Often you will find co-ops where parents share teaching responsibilities, host running clubs and hobby groups, or organize field trips.

Your state's homeschool organization will also be a hub for discovering what groups are available in your city. In addition, community centers may host homeschool events during the traditional school day, so it's worth contacting one in or two in your area. With any of those groups, focus on locating one homeschooler who will have a conversation with you about how they have built a homeschool community locally. Many are happy to do so.

Another option for some is to contact local churches and other religious organizations. Homeschooling historically has had robust networks in faith-based communities. If that's something you're open to exploring, call a few local churches in your area and ask to speak to the children's pastor. You can explain that you don't attend the church but are interested in connecting with homeschool families in the area, and ask the pastor for recommendations. I have done this every time we've moved to a new city and have never had a refusal. Pastors didn't ask me to tithe or become a member and they either connected me to homeschooling parents in their church or, if they didn't know any, recommended another local church that was more of a nexus. It's been a great resource.

Once you have found a parent to call, start by asking him a few questions about how his family is connected to local homeschoolers and groups. At the end of your call, ask if he knows anyone else you could talk to in the area. It's wise to go into these conversations knowing a few things.

First of all, plan to set aside time for a few phone calls with other homeschool parents in order to get a larger sketch of what groups and resources are available. Sometimes the information will overlap, which is a good validation of where circles of friends may be converging (and what might be a good starting point.) Ask parents what groups have been most life-giving to them, where they would recommend that a first time homeschooler start, and if they have suggestions for play groups and co-ops.

> Your state's homeschool organization will also be a hub for discovering what groups are available in your city.

Second, expect that as parents tell you about their groups they will likely express a great deal of warmth and pride in doing so. For each parent, their group will likely feel like the best group ever because it meets their family's needs. When homeschool support networks meet our needs, they begin to feel like extended family. But that's not to say that one family's group will also meet your family's needs. So try to find out:

- what that family likes best about the group
- what their kids are getting out of the group (socially/academically)
- how the group operates
- how the group enhances families' goals to homeschool
- a general idea of costs—memberships, fees, and time requirements

Third, as you take notes on these calls, encourage yourself to pick only one group to start. Maybe two. (More on that in a moment.) Just like when you entered high school and there were more activities than you had time to join, the same is true of homeschool groups. There will be speakers clubs, theater groups, rock climbing teams, choir, martial arts clubs, mock trial teams, sports, and more. Initially, it may be tempting to jam so many groups into your schedule that you don't have enough time to get schoolwork done—and it may begin to feel like you are living in your car.

Finally, look for online as well as in-person groups to join. Some groups are more active than others and they are often free, so it's a good idea to join a few until you find a good fit.

After you have officially joined the group, send an ISO ("In Search Of") email. It may sound cheesy, but I have done this every time we have moved to a new city with great results (and many other parents have too). Over email, I introduce our family to the list, say I have four kids with these ages who love Legos, Nerf, and scooters, and ask if anyone wants to meet at the park to play. It's not nearly as blind-date-ish as it sounds, and it's yielded some of my best life friends.

> Psychologists pointed out that parents often overstructured playtime and under structured academics.

In addition, online groups create a great network for shared community, resources, and access to possibilities you may not have considered—like a parent offering a free online class about Claymation to any homeschoolers who want to join. When searching for social groups, remember that online networks often extend beyond neighborhood boundaries, so keep looking until you find one that fits.

Especially during seasons of isolation brought on by weather, illness, or life changes, an online community can be extremely valuable. I reached out to our big group networks on a number of occasions during COVID-19, asking if anyone's kids wanted to meet up with mine to play impromptu Pictionary on Facetime, or online board games with a friend. My kids were also invited by other homeschool families to join free online, age-appropriate escape rooms with their friends. Be brave: Express your interest and need to your online homeschool community and see what happens.

THE VALUE OF PLAY GROUPS

When I began homeschooling our children, my first thought was to join a home-school science class (since I had loved mine so much as a tween.) At the time, I was looking for an academic co-op—something that would really challenge my

5- and 3-year-old sons and help them explore their world. What I stumbled onto instead turned out to be much better—a play group.

After a quick web search I discovered a homeschool play group (also sometimes called a "play co-op"— something that hadn't been invented yet in our area when I was being homeschooled), so I reached out to the coordinator and asked to meet at a park to find out more. Our four boys ran around the playground for two hours like we had filled their sippy cups with espresso (we hadn't), and Julie and I had a wonderful time getting to know each other. She was not only a delight, but also a great resource—answering a lot of my questions about homeschooling in our area. Over months and years she became one of my closest friends.

That day, Julie introduced me to the value of consistent, unstructured play. I did more research after meeting with her and found multiple published studies emphasizing the value and significant need for unstructured play for developing minds. Many psychologists pointed out how parents overstructured playtime (with organized sports and early access to technology) and often under structured academics (assuming their child's academic needs were covered in school).

While written about the traditional school model, the point was still relevant that, as parents, we were getting the two switched. Rather, we need to structure their work instead of their play, both alone and with friends, so their minds are free to be creative.

Despite strong, persistent findings, this idea has not yet fully caught on even within the homeschool community, and sometimes parents continue to under-prioritize play. Play is not just for preschoolers. The studies included students into high school as well. There are many play co-ops geared toward older students, so please seek those out too (my kids had a weekly indoor PE class in Seattle they adored, with lots of sweating teenagers running around in crazy group games).

Our play group turned out to be the highlight of the week—not just for the kids but for me. Not only did it release me from the burden of having to organize regular playdates (that so often got squelched last minute because someone got an ear infection or a strange cough), but it gave us dependable friends. Every Friday we showed up at a park for two hours to play with whatever friends from our group were there. Each group was organized somewhat geographically so none of us ever needed to drive more than 15 to 20 minutes to get to the park, and we rotated weekly through parks in our area.

Each group also aimed to limit membership to 12 to 20 families—large enough that there would always be kids to play with, but friends still noticed if we didn't show. We all knew each other's kids (and the kids knew all the parents), and it became a respite to meet, debrief, vent, laugh, suggest, relax, and help. I cannot imagine teaching at home without those families.

Especially beautiful was that each of us was coming from different education backgrounds, often had different academic goals for our kids, typically used different curriculum, and ran our schools at home differently. Whether it was despite those differences or because of them, we thrived together.

That's why I recommend a play group as your core group. It automatically invites opportunity for growth, flexibility, and much-needed support as you explore homeschooling. And if you need to change curriculums, not only do you have other parents on hand to query, you also don't have to change groups because this is play-based instead of curriculum-based. Plus, it's a fabulous incentive for finishing schoolwork so everyone can run around with buddies.

THE VALUE OF ACADEMIC CO-OPS

Unlike a Play Co-op, where families gather weekly for unstructured fun at local parks, Academic Co-ops create a regular meeting space for homeschooled students of a similar age to learn together in a classroom about a variety of subjects. Because of various moves, we have participated in six different academic co-ops over the years— some a better fit than others. For each of them, I was grateful that my kids already had a solid friend base before we joined because it accomplished two things. First, my kids were likely to have friends already at the academic co-op when we started (which helped them transition to the classroom setup quickly and easily). Second, if it turned out the co-op was not a good fit for us, it wasn't the end of the world if we switched to another.

As a former professional educator, I entered co-ops warily—especially those that were teaching core curriculum that I had signed on to teach at home. If I truly wanted an individualized learning experience over core content for my student, the only reason I would sign them up for a core class with 20 other students was if it was a subject I didn't feel capable of teaching myself.

Co-ops add value by providing courses that parents could otherwise not teach on their own—either because of the specificity or training behind the content or because the lesson is taught better with a larger group. Co-ops are meant to enhance our child's education, not replace it. My kids have loved taking extracurriculars in PE Games (which benefited from having more kids in class than what we have at home to play), Exploding Science (definitely don't want that in my kitchen), Spanish (I don't speak Spanish), Art Journals (I know very little about how to produce art), Improv (again, it helps to have a group), and Mock Trial (they actually brought in a lawyer to help, and it takes a group to pull it off). These are great examples of how a co-op can supplement the education you are providing at home. Sometimes there are core subjects at certain grade levels that parents feel ill-equipped to teach—that is a great time to involve an academic co-op into the weekly work flow.

Most co-ops require full-time parent participation; they are not drop-off programs. So plan to be involved as a teacher in classes (whether or not your child is in that class) as part of your membership requirement. My time teaching co-ops has been well spent as it has given me a breather from my standard homeschool routine, helped me think beyond our household, given my kids a new appreciation for Mom as their teacher, and kept a spark of fun in our week as the kids explore new topics. While it has not really been a place to make friends or develop deeper relationships (practically speaking, it is hard to make buddies when we are teaching a circle of 10 students how to become an eloquent public speaker). Frankly, that was never the goal. Play Co-ops are a place to play and connect with our friends, Academic Co-ops are a place to take classes with our friends and learn new subjects. Keeping our expectations clear on the distinct purposes of those groups helps us make sure we are meeting everyone's needs, academically and socially.

Should you need to switch groups, don't beat yourself up. Eventually, all our kids outgrow clothes, preferences, and fascinations. Continue to adapt to the need in front you and do your best to meet it as your child grows strong.

Remember to picture your children like a grove of fruit trees; each has a different trunk with its own bends, quirks, fruit, and shape. When the tree begins to produce fruit, the branches will need to be braced and the trunk supported so it can continue to grow straight and produce well. What you would do for one tree is not identical to what you would do for another. Anticipate that you'll have to rework your plan from time to time, and you will feel less discouraged when those alterations are required.

DEVELOP YOUR CORE

As hard as it sounds, after a month or so of getting to know groups in your area, try to identify a group that would be an excellent core, or anchor point, to your week. A core group is one that benefits all members of your family in some way, and is the one activity a week you are willing to schedule everything else around. After identifying your core group, begin to narrow down your other memberships to just two or three in order to protect your time schooling at home. Once you have established a rhythm, you can increase the number of groups you join, depending on the age of your students. Please remember—there are always more homeschool groups to join than time. Sometimes we say no to good options to create the best lifestyle for our families.

If your family includes a wide age range, address the needs of the older kids, as they tend to be more complex than the toddlers, who are probably just as happy with a bottle of bubbles.

If this is your first year homeschooling, prioritize groups that build friendships. Many studies have proven the value of play in a child's life; I realize I continue to beat this drum, but it requires beating. We might be tempted to sign our kids up for yet another Spanish or art class, when what they really need is two hours every Friday to meet up with a cluster of friends at the park to play tag, dodgeball, Nerf battle, and hide and seek. Remember that work must balance with play in our children's lives.

> Studies have shown time and again that open-ended, unstructured play reinforces creativity, innovation, leadership, and social skills.

Frankly, as parent teachers, we could do with some play time, too. As we discussed above, the more your circles overlap, the more frequently you'll see other parents and begin to form deeper friendships.

WHAT TO LOOK FOR IN A GROUP

There are oodles of types of homeschool groups. When searching for your core group I encourage you to look for a community with a flexible curriculum, meaning that being a part of the club will not require you to use a specific curriculum as your core subjects.

Curriculum-based co-ops can be a fantastic resource, and I know many families who have been very happy in them. However, tying yourself to a curriculum group as your core group to start may present a challenge later on as you get to know your child's learning preferences (see Chapter 6), or if you have another child and discover the required curriculum is no longer a good fit.

I have seen this play out before, where parents are faced with the hard decision of either customizing their children's curriculum or keeping their core community. As I think back on my own story as a homeschooled child, I recognize in hindsight (had one been available) that a structured educational co-op would have been great for me but cataclysmic for my brother—two kids raised by the same parents in the same home needing very different educational platforms. Every child learns differently. So absolutely join an academic co-op if it is a good resource for your family, but consider it secondary.

Balancing play with academics during the week is so important. Studies have shown time and again that open-ended, unstructured play reinforces creativity, innovation, leadership, and social skills. Just as it is important to attend academic co-ops that provide rigorous learning opportunities, it is equally important to create pockets each week for innovative play at the park with friends.

In looking for a group, I also look for perks—by that I mean, what can I do better as a part of this group than I could do by myself? For example, if I wanted to teach my kids basketball, it would be pretty difficult to do that without a full team, so we'd join a club so they can learn how to play that sport. Or if I'm the sort of parent who feels nervous about teaching science because I barely scraped by in high school, it's a great idea to join a science co-op. Yes, I know I just talked about not making an academic co-op the foundation of your social network, but that doesn't mean you can't add it into the mix. Joining a curriculum-based co-op is an excellent decision if it provides the support you and your children need.

Additionally, you will discover that socialization is easier when you overlap circles. Whenever I look for new groups, especially when moving to a new area, I try to find ways to overlap pockets of people we see during the week to deepen connections and build a community where we do life together. Once we have chosen our core group, I get to know other parents in that group and ask what else their families are involved in locally. From those conversations I learn about all kinds of possibilities, like a robotics club, a homeschool PE class, or a book club for teens.

By visiting those groups we then find natural overlap with the friends we were already developing in our core community, so that by attending three different groups a week we start seeing the same sets of friends over and over. It gives my kids a sense of being known and having friends.

Finally, in looking for a group, consider opening up to diverse perspectives. I believe it is important for us as parents to expose our children to life outside their community so they can see the world through someone else's eyes. It's easy for me to get trapped in my social bubble that only reflects me, and takes just a little intentionality and commitment on my part to get us out of that bubble.

One family I know joined a group of volunteers cleaning up parking lots and landscaping at local elementary schools before fall. Other families will drive an extra 20 minutes just to join a co-op that reflects a different background or perspective than their own. If you decide to do the same, you can then arrange playdates incorporating people in your core community with those in your new network—we do that through hosting a monthly Nerf battle for kids from across the city at a local park on Sundays. By reaching out in creative ways and spaces, we build opportunities for meaningful relationships that connect our children in authentic ways to people from different age, ethnic, or economic backgrounds.

IF YOU CAN'T FIND WHAT YOUR CHILD NEEDS

If local homeschool groups don't offer what your child needs, it's easy enough to start your own. After joining our first play group with my friend Julie, we moved away and I ended up starting play groups in our next two cities because what we wanted did not exist.

If you're considering starting a new group, here are a few ideas:

- organize a book club for teens, so they can get together monthly and discuss the same book with friends
- combine show and tell with some playdates with friends to give children an opportunity to develop public speaking skills
- trade hosting Arts and Crafts Days (sometimes with artist trading cards) at each others houses monthly to help children develop some kinesthetic and social creativity
- share organization of Field Trips With Friends, where each parent designs a field trip or two during the school year and get to see life behind the scenes at the dump and the fudge factory (you'll never guess which the kids thought was cooler!)
- organize Outdoor Fun, where we explore the architectural history of our city or go for a hike together
- share learning experiences, when one parent leads a series of animal dissections and another teaches the students every step of knitting from sheep to sweater

Having said all this, I recognize there are seasons in life when the social element is difficult for reasons beyond our control. It is in those seasons that it is especially important to be plugged in to an online homeschool community so that you feel connected and a part of something bigger than you. Oftentimes, online homeschool communities are an even easier place to meet your child's social needs. For creative ideas of how to develop social opportunities for you and your children if you are stranded at home, please check out the lesson in my video series, *Quick Start Guide to Homeschooling*.

EVERYTHING IS BETTER WITH A FRIEND

It really is. Homeschooling, too. While initially it may take some effort to locate families and groups that match up with your kids' ages and interests, they will breathe a tremendous amount of life into your homeschool journey.

5

Is Homeschooling Legal, And Will it Stay That Way?

Expert Help on Legal Questions

W hile nearly everyone agrees that children deserve a solid education, there are different viewpoints about the best way to legally provide it. Sometimes groups that seem to support the same goal suggest very different solutions. Before taking this conversation any further (and as long as we are talking about legal needs), I first need to include a disclaimer: *if you have specific legal questions about homeschooling you should contact your school district, state education department, or an attorney who specializes in this area to make sure you follow whatever legal guidelines exist in your district.*

We will start this chapter by addressing the basic questions around how to homeschool legally; the second part of this chapter will be devoted to keeping it that way.

In search of a holistic view of the legal issues surrounding homeschooling, I have interviewed and researched many sources from all sides of the discussion. My goal was to find areas of agreement among organizations so that together we can strive for educational excellence so that families can make informed decisions.

Among the many diverse sources, my research included the Homeschool Legal Defense Association (HSLDA), the National Home Education Research Institute (NHERI), and the Coalition for Responsible Home Education (CRHE). Many of the groups I researched believed in the need to offer an excellent education for homeschooled students, but had distinct approaches to doing so.

Homeschooling is legal in all 50 states in the U.S. (and in many countries). Every state has its own requirements to homeschool legally. Depending on your state, homeschooling legally is probably pretty straightforward. Sometimes it's as easy as filing a letter of intent with your local district.

> How you choose to educate your children at home will determine what legal steps you need to take.

In addition, how you choose to educate your children at home will determine what legal steps you need to take. Do you prefer the Private Home-school option, where you have high autonomy and authority over the process? Or Public Home-school, which is a hybrid public-private model? Doing online school at home through your local school district or a private school? Each of these scenarios requires a different first step.

(For further clarity on the four ways to homeschool, please see Chapter 2. Need more help? Our *Quick Start Guide: Video Series* offers a thorough overview of home-based education possibilities. If you have questions about your state's specific requirements, please look for *Links to Experts* on HomeschoolExpert.com.)

BACKSTORY

How homeschooling became legal is another story altogether. I had the opportunity to interview Mike Smith, President of HSLDA and one of the original lawyers who dedicated his career to expanding and protecting the freedoms of homeschoolers. HSLDA was formed in 1983 by Mike Farris and Mike Smith, when homeschooling was legal in just five states; thanks to the collective efforts of many, including those at HSLDA, homeschooling is now legal in all 50.

Back in the 1990s, many states were taking the position through their Departments of Education and local school districts that parents had to be certified teachers to legally educate their children at home. "That stance eliminated 85% to 90% of families from homeschooling," Mike Smith explained. "We knew that homeschooling was a wonderful opportunity for families to bond while educating and training their children well, so we began to look at what we could do to provide legal counsel and support to families who wanted to homeschool but were not professional educators." The goal of HSLDA, and other lawyers working alongside it, was to make homeschooling legal in every state.

In the early '80s, Smith recalled, "very few states were homeschool friendly. In fact, most were hostile. States like Iowa, Nebraska, North Dakota, and Texas were taking parents to jail if they homeschooled, arguing neglect and truancy, and threatening to remove the kids from their homes and put them in foster care."

It's hard to believe now, but I remember families in that era talking about staying indoors during school hours so that neighbors would not see the children—even though homeschooling was legal in their state—because it was largely misunderstood and often enough neighbors called the police on charges of truancy. Friends of mine recall being visited at home by police officers, their parents being questioned out front of the home, and lawyers from HSLDA stepping in to validate and protect the family's rights. Homeschooling was a different world then, which perhaps helps explain why families who homeschooled in the 1980s remain skeptical of involving the state in home education even now.

Though homeschooling is now legal nationwide, HSLDA continues its work to support families and homeschooling freedoms. "Our membership is available to anyone, no matter their faith perspective," Smith said. "We are clearly a faith-based organization, but we want to be open to the opportunity to serve parents from any belief system because we believe homeschooling is a parent's right. It's not just a *religious* parent's right, but *any* parent who wants to responsibly, lovingly teach their child at home. We support many freedoms at HSLDA, including the freedom to choose your own religion as a family and to instruct your children in whatever that religion may be as long as it is done in a safe, loving, legal way. In the last 10 years HSLDA has not lost a single legislative case when there have been attempts to reverse our freedom."

HSLDA also agrees it is not the only organization looking to protect the freedoms of homeschoolers in America, so feel free to select whatever legal supports best meet your family's needs.

THE CURRENT STATE OF HOMESCHOOLING

All that said, homeschooling is a different world now than it was in the '80s and '90s. In many states, the Department of Education is supportive of homeschoolers, offering "public school at home" (also called "charter schools" in some states), which is a hybrid model between private homeschooling and public education, providing teacher parents with support, accountability, and financial reimbursement. Among those who devoted their careers to seeing homeschooling legalized nationally, this hybrid model can sometimes elicit concern that parents are relinquishing hard-won freedoms. However, for those new to education at home, public homeschooling versus private homeschooling are simply two genuine options for teaching children. (See Chapter 9 for more information about both.)

In addition to becoming legal, there are three other considerations to keep in mind: truancy, state evaluations, and student ID cards.

TRUANCY

Truancy laws vary by state. Truancy is simply a legal term for a student being out of public school without the permission to be absent. As long as you continue to comply with your state's requirements to homeschool legally, truancy will not be an issue.

When I asked Mike Smith about truancy laws, he noted: "The legal response to this can be prosecution of parents and/or the family court can be enacted and petitions can be filed, and in that situation the allegation will be that the parents are neglecting the education of their children. No one wants that. So find out what you need ahead of time to homeschool legally in your state."

STATE EVALUATIONS

Many states require that families have their students evaluated by selecting from a list of standardized tests, or sometimes by submitting their child to a credentialed, independent third party to be evaluated through a portfolio of work and an interview. Typically, these evaluations are done at the end of the year and it varies by state how often you need to turn them in, if at all. Your state's evaluation requirements are available through *Links to Experts* on HomeschoolExpert.com

STUDENT IDS

It's a great idea to get a student ID card for any of your students who are older than 12 and who may have the opportunity to be on their own without you. This becomes especially helpful if your student has a job outside the home where she may be away from you during school hours. A student ID gives her official permission to be absent from a public school building during school hours if she is ever questioned. Giving your child a student ID card is another way to protect her, not to mention potentially get student discounts at various stores and attractions. Student ID cards can be printed free online and laminated at home, or purchased through online badge making companies.

THE STRONGEST SUPPORTERS

While HSLDA and other lawyers and organizations have done great work to advance the freedoms of parents to homeschool their children, many are quick to add that the strongest advocates in the pursuit to teach at home are not the lawyers but the homeschoolers themselves. Not because the homeschoolers have great influence, wealth, or power (very few do), but because families continue to engage in the court of public opinion by writing op-eds, calling their radio stations, visiting their representatives and senators, and writing letters to lawmakers when needed.

Mike Smith added a bit more historical perspective to this point: "When parents first earned the privilege to teach their own children at home legally in all 50 states, we did not need to motivate them to protect those freedoms. But we do see that beginning to change with the current generation of families entering into homeschooling for the first time, largely because they simply don't know what it took to get here." Smith and his colleagues encourage families to continue to remain attentive, engaged, and proactive in supporting the freedom to teach at home.

> I find that those most reactive to homeschooling often don't have an accurate perspective of what homeschooling really is.

WHY WOULD SOMEONE WANT LAWMAKERS TO RESCIND HOMESCHOOLING FREEDOMS?

I find that those most reactive to homeschooling often don't have an accurate perspective of what homeschooling really is. Sometimes that is due to lack of information, and other times misinformation. Once I provide clear information on what homeschooling is, how it is regulated, and how well homeschoolers perform when transitioned back into the traditional setting, many I am speaking to become more open to the idea.

Until recently, if the media ever provided coverage of homeschooling, it was in the rare case that perpetrators had used it as a guise for child abuse. I asked Mike Smith what his experience has been in such cases in the past. He told me: "We assert that the whole reason parents homeschool their children is because they love their children. We certainly don't want to see any child abused or neglected. Anyone that harms a child under the guise of false pretense—whether saying it is homeschooling or foster care or whatever other system—must go through due process and, if convicted, receive the full punishment to the full extent of the law. Absolutely." He added that we must be careful, as a society, not to assume that homeschooling is at fault for child abuse happening in the first place.

Smith continued: "There will be bad parents in anything, unfortunately. Traditional schools are not a panacea to prevent that. Child abuse happens to children no matter what school they attend—public, private, or homeschool— and there are even cases of abuse by teachers. But we don't blame the traditional school model for the abusive teacher or the abusive parent putting their child in public school. That would be illogical. How they broke the law is considered unrelated to their education philosophy. We must extend that logic to homeschooling also. Ultimately, we cannot prevent people from doing evil, we can only punish them if they do so."

The second reason some are against homeschooling is that they reject the data supporting the benefits of home education. The National Home Education Research Institute is an excellent start in looking at the data. The NHERI has been founded and run by Dr. Brian Ray since the early 1990s, "conducts and collects research about homeschooling ... and publishes a peer-reviewed research journal called the *Home School Researcher*. The NHERI specializes in homeschool research, facts, statistics, scholarly articles, and information" and is regularly called upon as an expert witness to legislators and in court.

Finally, some are against homeschooling because they believe that if parents teach about their own culture or faith at home, it might undermine the message being communicated in schools. The Coalition for Responsible Home Education (CRHE) is largely supportive of homeschooling but is primarily concerned with supporting the rights of the student to be culturally educated and academically evaluated on a regular basis in tandem with peers in the traditional school.

As I said in the beginning, many of us are pursuing the same goal of providing an excellent education for children, but we have different beliefs about the best way to go about it. While my state does not require me to evaluate my children every year, I chose to do so anyway (turning in results only on the years the state requests it) because I find the evaluations a helpful assessment tool for me as the teacher. Many other homeschooling parents do the same, going above and beyond what the state requires in content, assessment, and training. I believe parents want what is best for their children, and when that is within their power to do so with education, they will.

For more resources on how to homeschool legally, please look for Links to Experts at HomeschoolExpert.com

6

How Do I Discover How My Child Learns Best?

Studying Your Child

First of all, bravo to the parents asking this question. When I taught high school English, I desperately wanted to adapt every lesson plan to each of my 30 students across six class periods to meet their individual learning preferences. But as much as teachers want to reach every student, the honest truth is that we can't. We have to shoot for the majority. A tailor-made education is one of the perks that made homeschooling so attractive to me as a parent. But in order to customize your child's education to her individual learning preference, you first need to know what it is.

IDENTIFYING BASIC LEARNING PREFERENCES

While the theories on learning preferences are ever expanding and renaming themselves, there seems to be a consistent theme that divides learning styles into three main channels. That is not to say that a person will learn and communicate only through that one channel, but that a majority of the time—and for certain subjects or settings, especially—it is easier for all of us to access new information if it is presented in a way that aligns with our ideal learning preference. Of course, the more we engage all three learning preferences, the greater the likelihood the content will stick.

If possible, include your child in the process of understanding her learning preferences. Not only can it build her confidence, it may help you understand her better. (It did for me, when my son told me one day how his brain worked with grammar like it did with Legos.)

The following is an excerpt about learning preferences from my book *Study Smart, Study Less* (Random House, 2011). Written as a guide to help students from all ages and education backgrounds, its principles work well for elementary students through undergraduates. Because the book is written directly to the student, you might choose to read this part aloud to your child and then talk about it.

Everyone's brain works differently, and each person has one or two learning strengths that trigger a whole mental warehouse of storage space. Your brain is desperately hoping you will discover yours so that learning will become a lot more fun and a lot less work.

The first step to making learning easier is understanding what kind of learner you are. Before I launch into the different learning types, *first* take the 10 Q Test. Trust me, it's really important that you answer the questions *before* reading the rest of the chapter. And it's the perfect test because none of the answers are wrong. Just circle the choice that seems like the *best* possible answer for *you,* even though it may not be 100%-all-the-time-true. We're aiming for the answer that shows how you would react *most of the time,* and if your perfect answer isn't listed, just circle whatever is the next most likely answer.

1. You remember your new code or password best when
    a.) you say it aloud to yourself over and over again
    b.) you stare at the paper it's printed on and
        read it over and over again
    c.) you practice using it over and over again

2. If you were trapped in the waiting room at the dentist for half an hour you would probably
    a.) read a magazine
    b.) pace the room, drum on your knee with your fingers, or find some way to move around
    c.) listen to an audiobook or the background music piped into the waiting room and let your mind wander

3. If you were trying to remember where you left your library book you'd most likely
    a.) talk yourself through where you would have had it last
    b.) visualize yourself reading the book and then follow the mental steps where you set it next

c.) walk through the house and retrace your steps

4. To boost your confidence to try out for the lead part in theater club you might
   a.) go exercise or run around to burn off your jitters and build up courage
   b.) practice what you'd say aloud a few times to get comfortable with the words
   c.) write out a list of all the reasons the director would pick or pass you for the part, and what you need to do to get the lead

5. By the end of the semester, you tend to remember most easily the work that you
   a.) wrote down in math assignments, English paragraphs, or your science notebook
   b.) read from a school or library book
   c.) developed into a model, project, or experiment

6. If you wanted to learn how to make a perfect soft-serve ice cream cone (it's harder than it looks!) you would probably first want to
   a.) watch someone else make a soft-serve ice cream cone
   b.) try to make a soft-serve ice cream cone
   c.) listen to someone explain how to make a soft-serve ice cream cone

7. If you saw a car flatten someone's mailbox and tried to remember the license plate, your first instinct might be to
   a.) repeat the license plate number over and over
   b.) close your eyes and reenact what you saw in your mind to help you remember
   c.) write the license plate number in the air with your finger

8. If you heard a new song you liked and wanted to learn the lyrics, you'd most likely
   a.) read them while you listen to the song
   b.) sing them with the song while it plays, even if you bungle the words badly
   c.) just listen to the song on repeat and try to memorize the lyrics as you hear them

9. When your mom gives you instructions on how to take out the trash, you're more likely to remember and obey if you
   a.) picture yourself doing it while she talks
   b.) look at the floor and focus on what she's saying
   c.) look at her face while she talks

10. If you could design the perfect study environment it would most likely be

    a.) a comfortable temperature that enables you to stretch and move around

    b.) somewhere that has boring, steady background noise to block out other sounds

    c.) absolutely silent and well lit

HOW'D YOU DO?

The hardest part of this test, honestly, is adding up the totals correctly. Don't just sum the a's, b's, and c's. First, divide them like you see below and put the proper number of checks into each box.

QUESTIONS	A = Auditory	B = Visual	C = Kinesthetic
1			
3			
5			
7			

TOTALS: _____ _____ _____

QUESTIONS	C = Auditory	A = Visual	B = Kinesthetic
2			
6			
8			

TOTALS: _____ _____ _____

QUESTIONS	B = Auditory	C = Visual	A = Kinesthetic
4			
9			
10			

TOTALS: _____ _____ _____

GRAND TOTALS: _____ _____ _____

If your strengths don't fit neatly into one category, don't sweat it. Most people are a combination of two learning strengths. Your top score will show a *tendency* in your learning style, and if your top two scores are close in number it means you have two strengths to work with when learning something new. Lucky you. If you are evenly spread across all three groups, try practicing all three using different subjects and settings to see which works best—it's unlikely that you don't have a dominant learning strength and instead means I needed to ask you more questions.

CHARACTERISTICS OF LEARNING PREFERENCES

Learning preferences, also called learning modes or learning styles, tend to be divided into three primary types: Visual, Auditory, and Kinesthetic. (There are even more complex ways to categorize learning strengths using other methods, but for now we're sticking with the basics.)

Your score above will land you in one or two of the following categories, the descriptions of which should sound familiar. However, even if you scored highest in Kinesthetic doesn't mean that the entire Kinesthetic description will apply. You may even find glimpses of yourself in Visual and Auditory, as well.

So, then, what's the point? The point is to locate where you have your greatest strengths so that when it comes time to learn something new you can work *with* those strengths instead of *against* them. It's part of that *study smarter, not harder* idea. The easier it is for your brain to learn the material, the quicker you can finish, and the stronger your comprehension.

Auditory learners tend to do well in a traditional classroom setting because the information is presented in a format that naturally works well with her learning style. (That doesn't necessarily mean auditory learners will remember that new information without practice; it may just be easier to understand because someone explained it to her.) If you're an auditory learner you may remember people's names just from hearing them the first time or two, you might remember something better if you've said it aloud to yourself a couple of times, perhaps you hum or talk while you work, or you might be able to work well despite muted noise in the background.

Visual learners also tend to do well in a traditional classroom setting because they need to *see* it to get it. They learn best with diagrams, charts, pictures, textbooks, and written directions. If you're a visual learner, you may like having your to-do list written down, you might spend extra effort to make sure your notes are neatly written, and you might remember people's names better if you see them written on a name tag. Perhaps you close your eyes when you need to remember something in order to visualize it first, or you might especially need a quiet place to study to help you concentrate and hear your own thoughts.

Kinesthetic learners, unlike the other two, tend to dislike the traditional classroom setting. In fact, the idea of sitting at a desk and taking notes just about crushes his spirits. What these students need is hands-on learning, such as performing science experiments, building models, acting in plays, or creating something with glue and toothpicks. If you're a Kinesthetic learner you might understand directions better if you visualize yourself performing them instead of just reading them silently. Whether or not you are aware of doing so, you might tap, draw, or tinker when you're bored, use gestures when you speak, be skilled with creating or building with your hands, or remember conversations based on how and where someone was standing at the time. Or perhaps having a hand fidget (or crocheting granny squares) will help you focus when someone is speaking. It may take a little extra creativity to find ways to get physically engaged with your schoolwork, but it is possible.

Whatever your score, it might interest you to know that 20%–30% of students are Auditory, 40% are Visual, and 20%–30% are Kinesthetic. There are no oddballs when it comes to learning strengths, though traditional schools may make Kinesthetic learners feel that way. In fact, researchers believe that some people who have been diagnosed with attention-deficit hyperactivity disorder (ADHD) have been incorrectly labeled. It turns out many were simply Kinesthetic learners who were struggling to focus in a class geared only toward auditory learning. Modern classrooms now make a greater effort to reach students across all three learning preferences. Having said all that, let me be perfectly clear: the Kinesthetic learning style is NOT a learning disability—it's a strength.

In addition to the 10 Q Test, a great way to study how your child absorbs information is through observing how he learns new chores. By removing your discovery process from an academic context, your results may be more authentic to your child's true nature. Studying how he learns using chores as a test is also helpful for temporarily setting aside the variable of some special learning needs. When you give your child a new job, pay attention to which communication style results in the best follow-through. Does he need it written down? Does he want to walk through the motions? Does he want to hear you explain it? Initially he may use all three, but over time his follow-through will likely show that one is predominant.

As you develop a theory about your child's learning preferences, test out that theory by practicing some accommodations with his schoolwork. Nearly all curricula can be modified in some way to meet your child's needs, especially if you think about applying learning outside of a traditional format. For math, a Kinesthetic learner will do much better with manipulatives—and that's just a fancy word for counting with beans or blocks, anything small that you have on hand. (If you want to astound your early elementary school child, do math with chocolate chips.)

When studying spelling, Auditory and Kinesthetic learners may do better by saying each letter in the word as they throw a ball back and forth, activating that part of their brain through movement. Older students might go back to making good old-fashioned flash cards when trying to memorize definitions or equations. (The act of handwriting, color coding, and flipping the cards activates the brain on a number of levels.). Also consider ways to incorporate assistive technology into whatever curriculum you have purchased.

If you or your student want to dig deeper into how to apply learning modes to all different kinds of study techniques, please check out *Study Smart, Study Less* for more practical tips.

CREATING A WORKSPACE THAT ENCOURAGES FOCUS

While some students may be more inclined to move or stand while they learn and others may be more easily distracted by the sound of the washing machine running in the other room, it is important to give all students the following:

SPACE AND ROUTINE

The mind is a creature of habit. We have spent a lifetime training it that the bed is where we sleep. It should not come as a surprise, then, that if your student decides to read his history book in bed he will get sleepy and find it difficult to concentrate. For the same reason, I found it incredibly helpful in college to go to the library to work—not because I needed to borrow books, but because it put me in a smart headspace and made it easier for me to buckle down and get work done.

When at home, it is helpful to have a routine with your learning space that will switch your child's brain over to student mode. For our family, that is the kitchen table. After breakfast we meet at the same time every morning (or as close to it as we can get) for Morning Meeting to discuss the day. After a quick chore break at the end of the meeting, the kids bring their school boxes to the kitchen table and we get started. I use this pattern to establish for their brains that we are at the table to work, not to eat.

Someday my children may read this book and realize I have been strategically and psychologically manipulating their environment and routines to help them stay focused and be successful; for now, it just feels like school—and that works for me. Simplify your workspace by avoiding snacks during school so that it is clear when you are sitting at a school table versus a meal table. (Plus, snacks make a great incentive to finish the lesson and take a break.)

> It is helpful to have a routine with your learning space that will switch your child's brain over to student mode.

In case you are suspicious of my tactics, know that I learned from one of the best: Mr. Rogers. Psychologists have actually dubbed this intentional transitioning between work and play the "Mr. Rogers Effect" in honor of the way Fred Rogers would begin every episode by trading his loafers and blazer for sneakers and a cardigan, to show that he was ready for play. Don't feel like your morning routine needs a lot of fanfare— simple is best. Loafers, boxes, or assignment books used consistently over time will help your children develop a work mindset that defines their role (and yours) during different hours of the day.

I know one mom whose child struggled to understand when she was in teacher mode versus when she was in mom mode, so she would wear a special hat during school hours to show when she was the teacher and it was time to do school. Whatever it takes. As tempting as it will be to let your children stay in their pajamas all day or do their math homework in the tree house, resist. It will make your job as teacher that much easier if they come dressed and ready to their workspace to behave, think, and work like students.

QUIET

The brain focuses best with quiet. It is as simple as that. Studies have shown that listening to certain types of classical or jazz music before beginning work can stimulate synapses and positively influence transitions. And while students often claim listening to music helps them study better, what it actually does is pass the time so they feel like they are getting more accomplished. In reality it costs extra effort for their brains to tune out the tunes. To the extent you can, keep your workspace quiet during your most critical school hours.

This principle extends beyond music. In the early years, our child Sam struggled with the distraction of the soft hum of our dishwasher when we schooled at the table after breakfast. I am ashamed to admit that even after a couple months of this, my response was to tell Sam to focus harder—I didn't know then what I know now about Sam. With time, I came to appreciate Sam's unique learning strengths, and I either left the dishwasher off during school or handed out some noise-canceling headphones to help block out the distraction. Use sound and soundlessness to your advantage to prep your students to learn as well as to free them to play and dance.

THE SCHOOL BOX

Whether a box or a basket, get each of your children their own container for storing individual school supplies and textbooks they can use every day. I encourage something with handles to make it easier for them—not you—to carry it to their workspace.

Occupational therapists have found positive connections between easily distractible students and heavy lifting exercises. Basically, when students are losing focus or struggling to stay on task, OTs recommend that they carry books from one side of the classroom to another to help organize, lug a laundry basket, or do push-ups against the wall. In our case, they carry their school boxes to the table from the hall closet to engage their brains. (My gym teacher would feel so vindicated right now).

My mom homeschooled my two brothers and me and used to say there were some days when she just needed to hand my brother a shovel and send him outside for a few hours. Other homeschool parents say their most significant focus tool is their trampoline. The bottom line here is to think creatively about ways you can get your child to do cross-body motion, pulling, pushing, and lifting so you can get his brain engaged and get back to work. Body movement is good for the brain.

Your child's school box should include a little container where she can keep all her school supplies. You will be amazed how quickly your quiet workspace can disintegrate when one child can't find her ruler and all the kids rush from the table to eagerly help her locate it. (If only they were so eager to help each other do chores *outside* of school time!)

Keeping your supplies all in one place will help you get through your school day efficiently. (Expert Tip: I give each of my kids a bundle of their own individual color of pencils each school year. That way, when I find pencils rolling on the floorboard of my car, I know who to send to clean them up.) We have even extended the school box idea to a To-Go Box version with a clipboard and mini zipper pouch so that we can finish up little assignments when needed at an eye doctor appointment, having everything ready but excuses.

I extend the school box to myself as well. My teacher box includes answer keys, lesson plans, my own box of supplies, samples of all the different kinds of paper I might need for each level of student, maps, timers, and whatever else helps me stay present with my students. Forcing myself to minimize in a box helps me focus on the work at hand rather than feel overwhelmed by the shelf of all the haven't-done-yets. Each of us is in charge of transporting, cleaning, and maintaining our own boxes. When boxes get messy, I add that to the assignment books so my students learn to value order in their workspaces.

CREATIVE TOOLS

In addition to the school box, let's build on that a step further and talk about creative learning tools. Some of my students have been able to study, remember, or focus better simply by customizing their tools. Consider supplying inexpensive pencil grips to help the pencil fit your daughter's hand, or a slant board so her papers are at the right angle for writing clearly. If your son struggles with focus, there are many different kinds of quiet fidgets he can keep under the table and save for school only. Some of my students who have struggled with anxiety while learning have benefited from a weighted vest or blanket. And, of course, make sure your child is properly seated at the table, either by providing a smaller table to fit his frame or a booster seat to elevate him to the right level. These are small changes that can have a big impact.

TIME

One of the most motivational tools in my teacher box is my attention. It's terribly tempting to text the outside world or surf the web while the kids do their work—I admit I struggle with it. But our children are so much more motivated when we keep our eyes on them: when we walk around behind her to see her work, place an encouraging hand on his shoulder, or put a kiss behind her ear. It means so much to them to feel seen and noticed when they are struggling with something as seemingly irrelevant to life as diagramming sentences.

Your nearness is also a chance to bond as you work together through the miserable and the marvelous. Love covers a multitude of troubles. Your attention is motivational because it helps your child feel seen and noticed while studying.

So do your best to guard your time from outside distractors, like those random appointments that like to pop up. When doctor's receptionists learn you are homeschooling and their eyes light up in the hopes you can take the 10:00 a.m. spot, decline it. Unless it is a specialist or a special occasion, I proactively block 8:00 a.m. to noon every day for school. It is worth all the self-discipline required to protect that time. Afternoons are then open to finishing individual work for the older students, play, activities, errands, or chores.

BREAKS

Everyone needs a break. You too. After you have focused on your children at the table for 15 to 20 minutes, take a break. If your child can only focus for 10 minutes, start there. Over time, you can increase his focus. Some days will require more flexing than others in the number of

> One of the most motivational tools in my teacher box is my attention.

breaks your child needs, and everyone is allowed to have an off day—I know I do. I like to use my 10-minute breaks to refill my coffee, return a call, throw a load in the wash, and set out the ground turkey to defrost for dinner—sometimes all in the same break. I encourage using a visual timer so students of all ages and abilities can easily track for themselves how much time remains in their break.

I like to toss in chore breaks during our morning as well as outside play—it's good to mix it up. The action of turning over laundry and carrying a clean basket upstairs may not be a hoot of fun, but it gets their muscles engaged (back to that heavy lifting principle we mentioned earlier) and gives them a little break from the subject without losing them completely to recess, when I sometimes spend just as much time getting them back to the table as we spent on math.

Over time, try to establish a pattern of school, chore, school, recess, school, chore, school, recess/lunch. Sometimes when I have a lot of work to do, the most efficient thing I can do is schedule my next break.

CUSTOMIZATION = YOU ARE IN CHARGE

Remember that you are in charge of your child's curriculum, especially if you have chosen to homeschool privately. (If you don't know what I mean by homeschooling privately, please refer to Chapter 2.) By educating your child at home, you get to determine when she has mastered the content and can move on. There is no need to drill and kill a point she had solid a week ago. If she got it, skip the extra problems and go forward. Certainly, review what she has mastered—a little every day—so she doesn't lose her mastery of the concept.

Curriculum companies are typically very generous with the number of problems on a page because they realize some students need more practice than others, some classroom environments require multiple sets of problems, and teachers assign homework differently. It is not unusual for math teachers in a traditional classroom to hand out a page of 15 problems, assign students numbers 1 through 12, evens—and then instruct them to skip the rest.

> There is a fair bit of trial and error when we study our children—we are, after all, working with human beings, and children at that.

That said, if you find you have worked all the problems with your child and she is still struggling with the content, do not skip to the next concept just because you ran out of pages. If she doesn't get it, try a new way of learning the material—a different learning preference and maybe a different curriculum just for that section—and keep working at it.

As you customize your child's education, along with adapting curriculum to his learning preferences and speed, look for ways to leverage his fascinations. If your daughter is fascinated by military planes, shape her learning around the topic. Find literature that explores it. Study the physics of flight. In math, create story problems that include flight plans, weight of shipments, and transportation time. Have her research the invention and evolution of the plane, and where it fits in the context of history. Have her write a paragraph or essay, depending on her age, about how the airplane led to modernization. The big takeaway is to customize your lessons to your student's interests, strengths, and needs to make learning meaningful and memorable.

IF VS. WHEN/HOW

There is a method of education called "unschooling," which often allows students to choose IF they learn the material—that is not what I'm talking about. At least for our family, we believe that some subjects are not optional—like reading or division. While the subjects may not be optional, the timing for learning them can certainly be flexible.

There is such a thing as forcing a child into a subject before she is ready, which will not only be frustrating for you both but ineffective. This point is most pronounced when talking about reading. Some of my children read from a very young age, but one did not. Every six months I reintroduced the material to see if she was ready for it, and when it brought on panic attacks I gave it another six months. She is now a voracious reader. It just took her a little longer to get there.

With other subjects, there is slightly less of a time buffer. If the state expects your child to master multiplication in fourth grade, you should make that your aim and seek outside help if he continues to struggle with the concept over the course of the year. That can sometimes be an indicator that you need to switch curriculum, which we cover in Chapter 8, or in rare cases might indicate a learning disability, which we discuss in Chapter 11.

There is a fair bit of trial and error when we study our children—we are, after all, working with human beings, and children at that. I encourage you to be flexible about when your child is ready to learn a skill or concept. Try, take a pause, and try again—without fear. State standards often allow an extended amount of time as a buffer for students to develop mastery in reading, understanding that many children learn to read at their own pace. If after two or three attempts to teach your child to read you are still running into trouble, reach out to your district or homeschool community for professional resources. It's not *if*, but *when* and *how* our children learn.

PUSHING, PULLING & MISTAKES

As homeschooling parents, we wear a lot of hats. Sometimes I call myself the sheriff—shoving my kids into what's good for them when I know they may not enjoy it in the moment but will benefit and appreciate it in the long run. Sometimes I call myself the teacher—pulling them into a new concept or idea with the creativity, interest, and excitement of the Pied Piper. Sometimes I feel like Mom—bringing up what we learned days or even months ago when some random situation arises in our lives, or reviewing some hard-earned principle or life lesson as any parent would no matter where his child goes to school.

Admittedly, sometimes it is difficult to know which hat to wear in a given situation. Over the years I have leaned heavily on wisdom beyond my own to guide me in the push and pull of growing each of our kids. It goes back to that tree metaphor I explained in Chapter 2. Each of our children is their own tree meant to produce their own fruit, and as a sapling it's unclear what that fruit will be. It's my goal to creatively support, nurture, and feed that tree what I think it needs, asking wisdom from other gardeners and the Maker of trees to figure out what is best. That doesn't mean I haven't made mistakes—I have. But amid this very practical chapter about learning modes and how we learn best, permit me to philosophize for just a few paragraphs more.

We began this lesson talking about learning modes. So let's talk about the biggest learning mode we often ignore: making mistakes. We have all made them. What a gift to our children to establish a healthy response to making a mistake, to be patient with ourselves, and to learn from what we did wrong. Our family's code is that if you make a mistake, you own up to it, learn from it, and move on—with the hope that with practice we will repeat that mistake less often. Perfectionism stifles learning.

> Plan to not get homeschooling exactly right the first time—no one has.

We cannot learn if we are unwilling to make some mistakes along the way. It takes a great deal of trial and error to study how our children learn best, so I encourage you to model grace to your child by first giving it to yourself. Plan to not get homeschooling exactly right the first time—no one has. Just when we think we have it figured out for all of time, the child changes, matures, sprouts a new limb, and we have to jury-rig the system to fit. And since no two kids are alike, what worked for one may or may not work for the other.

Simply by being here with me, you are actively learning from the mistakes of so many other homeschooling parents who eventually figured out how to make it work. Incorporating the learning tools we have discussed into your workspace will lead to a significant increase in focus and success, and will make learning together much more fun.

DIFFERENT TREES

In your willingness to learn as you go, continue to celebrate the principles of discovery. Of sitting down next to your child, identifying where he is struggling and frustrated, making note of how much time he can focus on a task before he mentally leaves the building, and then working with *who you discover he is*—not who you think he should become.

This is where having your family goals close by can be a source of encouragement—to see your stretch goals of where you are headed, the baby steps you are aiming to take this year or month, and what is on the agenda for this week and for today.

"One day at a time" has gotten me through some of the more sandpaper-like days of rubbing up against my children's uniqueness. Learning to lead them has refined *me* at times just as much as it has them by teaching me to see a perspective other than my own—when I set aside my own preferences and instead consider their needs, I find ways to validate and value them for their differences.

Just because I don't learn the way they do doesn't mean they are less than me—it just means we are different trees. And in the forest of life, diversity is a beautiful thing. Your unique style of applying these principles will be different for your family than they are for mine, and that is what makes me so excited about helping equip you to homeschool like an expert.

7

How Much Time Does It Take to Homeschool?

Designing an Effective Learning Routine

W ell, we are finally here. The long-awaited, much-anticipated chapter with all the nitty gritty tools that will make teaching at home easier. These are the handlebars you've been waiting for. This is the gold that has been mined from years of experience translating education methods from the traditional classroom to the homeschool environment by myself and many other homeschool experts. This is the wheel you don't want to reinvent. This chapter will be a long answer to a short question, but it will be worth it.

FLEXIBLE STRUCTURE

One of the most frequently cited reasons why parents love homeschooling is that it is flexible and adaptable. So as we talk about a typical day and how to make learning at home easier, let's start there. If you are new to educating at home, or new to incorporating structures into your homeschooling, setting super-clear expectations will make this transition easiest for everyone.

In other words, write them down.

Our personalities tend to prefer either structure or flexibility, but we can't ignore the one we dislike. They really work best together.

Across a range of disciplines, from military protocol to special-needs education, the same principle applies: Structure creates a clear purpose, a sense of calm, and a pathway for collaboration.

Still, when it comes to homeschooling, our structures must be built to flex. Your family is not my family, your needs are not my needs, your kids are not my kids. I expect that you will adapt the structures I share in this chapter to your family's needs—that is the beauty of bespoke learning. Likewise, I hope we can celebrate how all families educate in the way that meets their needs best.

This chapter is full of excellent structures that make homeschooling easier. If structures are not your favorite flavor, please don't have an allergic reaction—do your best to read the chapter, step away, and see what settles. If you think flexibility is terrifying and out of control, please don't marry your structures; your kids may be wired differently from you and will need breathing room. The more we all flexibly use structure in our day, the better the day will roll.

A STUDIOUS ENVIRONMENT

In Chapter 6 we devoted time to how your child learns best and what sort of environment will support her learning. This chapter takes those concepts a step further. While you don't have to turn your garage in a classroom or salute the flag at breakfast, it definitely helps to put some student supports in place.

Especially in the early years, when you are laying a foundation in math and reading, it is critical that you sit beside your student to supervise his work. The goal of this is to catch mistakes early before they become a toughened pattern, to keep him moving quickly through the page before he loses steam, and to provide immediate feedback and encouragement as needed. Too often, we treat our elementary students like small adults, handing them an assignment and sending them off to their rooms full of toys with the expectation they will complete it. While you can train your children to be self-taught (it is one of our education goals as a family), independent learning is a lesson on its own beyond the curriculum.

So while laying critical early foundations around phonetic blends, basic spelling rules, long division, and borrowing, work closely alongside your students. And protect your school space as best you can from noise and outside interruptions. We have never had an official school room; our kitchen table has worked fine. But it has definitely required flexibility on my part regarding the timing of breakfast dishes or the intentionality of meal prep.

SCHOOL SUPPLIES

Beyond the obvious requirements of curriculum and workspace, devise a way to keep your materials together. If you don't have much room for schooling other than the kitchen table (as we didn't), keep bins in a closet that your children can easily bring to the table each morning. Dollar stores are a great source for cheap storage, organization, and school supplies.

Be sure the learning space is well lit and, strangely enough, not too comfy—you want their brains to register that this is a workspace, not a lounge. Remember Mr. Rogers and stay away from beanbags and treehouses during school time. Find a way to keep charts handy, either hidden on the inside of cabinets or in a miniature version you can pull out as needed. Also, consider investing in some noise cancelling earmuffs if you have multiple students to help de-emphasize sibling conversations, especially as you go around the table throughout the morning to talk with each of them.

For my own mental well-being, it was a significant help to establish visual boundaries so I didn't feel like I was living in a classroom. It would have been too easy to get burned out as a nonstop teacher if I was staring at charts for parts of speech while making dinner every night. Keeping our supplies out of sight when not in use helped me maintain a healthy boundary between school and home.

It is critical that you sit beside your student to supervise his work.

In addition to organization supplies, our dollar store regularly sells packets of reward certificates. In the early years, when addition was harder and motivation was easier, it was fun to hand these out to the kids on occasions when I thought they had really pushed past their frustrations or challenges to reach a goal. I'd typically present them during dinner with fanfare in front of my husband, and it went a long way to boosting morale. We would hang it on the fridge for the next week, in view from the table, so my son or daughter could see it, pluck up their courage for the next problem, and get to it.

CHORE BOARDS

There are two buzzwords that have become popularized in parent circles and that I believe are connected: entitlement and resilience. No one wants to raise an entitled child, and parents often seek creative ways to boost their children's awareness of others' needs, stewardship of the environment, gratefulness, and sense of belonging in the family.

(*Wait a minute, I thought we were talking about school supplies ... is this a book on parenting now?* Well, yes ... as a parent teacher the two worlds overlap at times. Hang in there; I promise this will lead back into developing your student in a moment.)

Similarly, many parents want their children to be resilient—to stand up to a challenge, express confidence in the face of uncertainty, push past difficult circumstances to achieve a goal, and measure the value of something not on the effort required to get there but the value of the prize itself.

Chores help in both of those areas. Beyond simply getting your house clean (which, let's be real for a moment, would probably be cleaner if you did all the jobs yourself, at least in the early years), requiring your children to partake in regular household chores instills a work ethic and independence. It's especially key that their chores are not only about cleaning up *their own* messes but helping the household as a member of the family. At our house we call them "Team Crossman" jobs.

Before launching into a conversation on incentives, I will acknowledge that this is a personal topic for many parents—it's up there with pierced ears, how to discipline, and who pays for gas money. So please hear the heart behind what I'm saying and then apply it as it best fits your family's needs.

Privileges are not a guarantee; they have to be earned in our household.

In the early years, our kids earned zero allowance, tech time, or prizes for doing chores. Chores were just a basic requirement of being on our team. And there is no bargaining at our house about which chores they want to do and don't want to do. I can't think of the last time I have earned anything for keeping my house clean, beyond the satisfaction of a clean house.

While I am all about incentivizing in other areas of life (and we do!), when it comes to chores, we made it clear to our kids early on that they are a valuable member of our team, that we need their help, and that work is non-negotiable. (Which helps undermine any sense of entitlement.)

To support their growth in this area, we establish benchmarks along the way—for example, being able to take on a higher-level task means earning an extended amount of freedom or privilege in another area of life as part of growing up and earning trust. We believe that with responsibility comes privilege, and without opportunity for growth or advancement we remove the incentive to work.

But it takes a few years to get there. Especially in the early years—when it takes three times as long to coach a child through the job, circle back to check their progress, correct and redirect their efforts, and after multiple iterations and 30 minutes finally finish cleaning one bathroom mirror—I am not paying anyone.

That said, somewhere around age 8 to 11, depending on the child, we have told them that if they consistently complete their jobs the right way *without being asked* (underline that last part!), we believe they have earned a modest allowance of either money or additional tech time. At any point, though, if they consistently need reminders or fail to do the job well, we can revoke the privilege until they again prove themselves. Privileges are not a guarantee; they have to be earned in our household.

Whether you like chore sticks, charts, boards, or maps is up to you. I've tried every variation I could find over the years. What worked for us is consistent expectations and accountability. What that meant practically was a whiteboard for each of our kids that listed their chores for the day so they could check them off as they completed them. (Expert tip: I used wet-erase markers to write the chores and gave them dry-erase markers to add check marks; that way, the chores didn't "disappear" but were still easily modified.)

Team Crossman: Chores

DISHES & CLEAN KITCHEN

- All food away
- Counters tidied and wiped
- No trash
- Leftover dishes rinsed and stacked in sink

If dishes are not done by time deadline, must do next meal too (Parents reserve the right to rescind for extenuating circumstances).

Breakfast	Lunch	Dinner
EVELYN (Done by 10am)	**ISAIAH** (Done by 2pm)	**JOSIAH & EVANGELINE**

JOSIAH	ISAIAH	EVELYN	EVANGELINE
• Team Laundry (fold & away) • Set Table (nightly) • Trash/Recycle: Take out without being asked, includes trash day • Tidy Car (THU)	• Vacuum: Every night hardwoods; carpets (MON) • Mom Helper (ask!) • Organize Helper (TUES/THU) • Sister Helper: With love; includes supervising bird	• Dog: Scoop & feed (daily), bathe (SUN/THU) • Deck/Porch Tidy: Sweep (TUE) • Windows: Clean dog smudges (MON) • Tidy Commons & PR (Daily)	• Library Books: Organize & bag • Lysol handles & switches (TUE) • T.P. in all bathrooms (MON) • Clean ½ bath (THU)

Behind one of my cabinet doors was a list of the chores they were responsible for that quarter, since not every job needs to be done daily. Sometimes we overcomplicate tracking and rewarding chores. (And let's be real, it is hard enough to teach our children to clean in the first place, so let's not make the system any harder on the parents than it needs to be.) A reusable check sheet slipped in a plastic page protector is a simple and effective tool that can be crossed and wiped many times over. And for my helpers too young to read, I have put little icons next to their jobs on the list. By the end of the day, they need to have their chores done before they join us for family games, movies, tech, or dessert.

On page 101 is an example of chores at our house: For an entire quarter at age 12, Isaiah was responsible for vacuuming the downstairs every evening, breakfast dishes daily, a "Mom Helper" job daily, cleaning the toilets weekly, cleaning the bird cage weekly, and washing the windows inside weekly. Those were his Team Crossman jobs.

> Learning to balance chores with school and friends is a great time-management skill to develop early.

Beyond that, he was responsible for cleaning and putting away his laundry weekly (including changing his bedding), daily cleaning his room, completing his schoolwork, practicing piano, and tidying his belongings around the house. All this was kept on the chart inside the cabinet, and each morning I marked on his board any additional jobs I wanted him to complete that day. (Expert tip: If wet-erase markers don't work for you, try permanent markers for long-term tasks; you can always remove the permanent ink later with lemon oil).

By the end of the quarter, Isaiah had gotten better at cleaning toilets and vacuuming floors because of the consistent practice, and was encouraged to know that he would get to trade some of those jobs with a sibling once he mastered them so that he wouldn't have to do them forever.

This system works so much better for us than picking random chores from a bowl or shuffling them daily because it gives my children the opportunity to improve on a skill with consistent practice, keeps everyone accountable to not living like a maid will show up after the kids go to bed, and encourages fairness with the jobs rather than luck of the draw. (It also makes it easy to know who is responsible for my backyard being sprinkled with dog "presents" and to follow up with the child in charge of scooping instead of playing the "not me" game.)

With Team Crossman jobs, do my kids feel entitled? Not if I can help it. They know they are valuable members of our team, that we need them to pull their weight, and that privileges are optional and must be earned.

Are they resilient? We are working on it. Nothing builds resilience like asking your 9-year-old to clean the same bathroom mirror over and over and over to teach her the principle that the job is not done until it is done right. I'm not talking about perfection (which leaves no room for error); I'm talking about excellence (which expects the best someone can do given tools and circumstances). There is a difference. The independence my children learn from being able to manage their home, schedules, and lives eventually translates into a confidence that extends into academics.

(*Here we go: She is bringing it back to school!*) And by practicing this stick-to-itiveness with chores rather than school, I don't have to fight against negative self-talk like, "I'm too stupid to understand math." Almost anyone can learn to clean a mirror well with practice. We practice the art of doing something well outside of school so that, eventually, it translates back into school as well.

CHORES BY AGE

For parents feeling inspired to reconsider chores at home, I have included at the end of the book a suggested list of age-appropriate chores. (Just so my lawyer can sleep at night, this is where I add that adults should always supervise their children, especially when chemicals and kitchens are involved ... but you already knew that.)

Our kids are almost never too young to help in some way; encourage them regularly as they attempt a new skill, and remind yourself that if a 6-year-old is cleaning the bathroom sink, it will probably look like a 6-year-old cleaned the bathroom sink. Find the balance of guiding him through the process of learning to clean and seeing areas for improvement without crushing his soul.

And if you decide you absolutely can't stand the streaks he left behind, please oh please wait to clean them when your kiddo isn't looking; he was probably doing his best, no need to undermine his attempts.

My mom always told me that her goal with us as kids was to work herself out of a job. The Age Appropriate Chore List would be incredibly daunting were you to wait until your child is 11 to start. But if you begin early and tackle a skill every few months, her knowledge base will add up quickly and will be worth gold later on. I encourage you to help her master all the jobs before freshman year of high school when sports and extracurriculars tend to intensify the schedule. Learning to balance chores with school and friends is a great time-management skill to develop early.

It may be tempting to chuck the assignment book under the category of "stuff we don't need now that we are homeschooling" but I counsel you to consider otherwise. From a big-picture perspective, each student learning to manage her own assignment book is a practical life skill—a school subject all its own. Colleges directors have told me that, too often, they hear from professors and RA's that incoming freshmen arrive completely unpracticed at managing their own calendars; freshmen are used to parents charting their weekly activities for them and telling them what time to leave the house to get to practice, or how soon to begin work on a project that's due in three weeks.

Just as with chores, build up to time-management independence with your children by practicing from a young age with their assignments. The kids love the sense of accomplishment as they cross off what they have completed each day. Castaways and POWs have all had their way of etching survival hashmarks to buoy their spirits. Your kids (and you!) need it too.

Quite simply, an assignment book is a calendar. I have purchased inexpensive month-per-page assignment books at dollar stores for our early elementary students, and more extensive week-per-page assignment books as they mature and take on more subjects.

Chart assignments in your elementary student's book only a week at a time, since sometimes there are minor tweaks to the schedule along the way. The best time to organize their assignment books is before the week begins. There have certainly been Mondays I have woken up to realize that I never filled in their books, so I list off Monday's work while they eat breakfast and fill in the rest later.

Use your assignment books for more than just assignments. If you know your junior high student has an orthodontist appointment, or a visit from grandparents, or a soccer tournament, tell him Monday morning so he can put it in his assignment book. (Obviously, doctor's appointments will be overkill for most elementary students, but it is still helpful to add holidays and breaks into their books so they get used to merging work with the bigger life picture.)

Assignment books have saved my bacon on more than one occasion. Life is full of unexpected alterations—a dishwasher leaking all over the floor, migraine, neighbor emergency—and it has been incredibly useful to know that when our best-laid plans are thrown out the window the kids still have enough direction on their own to get them started. Even if in their math lessons they are only able to get to their review for that day and save the new work to do with me when I am freed up, that is better than having accomplished nothing. Fortunately, those desperate moments are rare. More commonly, I find assignment books to be helpful when pacing an overwhelming subject for a child, helping her break a large project into manageable chunks, keeping her accountable to work before play, and helping her look forward to an upcoming event so she can be ready to experience it to the fullest.

During elementary school, I fill in each week's assignments and expect the kids to check off each item as it is completed to make sure the work is done before Legos. In junior high, I work with our children to chart out their assignments—teaching them how to pace the year using the table of contents based on when they want to finish, how to tell when a quiz is coming up, and where to write all that in the book; at this point, I put 60% or less of their assignments into the book and they write the rest with my supervision.

By the end of eight grade, I expect our kids to manage 100% of the assignments in their

Use your assignment books for more than just assignments.

book as I dictate them. In other words, I am prepping them for a traditional classroom by saying, "This week I want you to be finished with lesson 86 in biology, math page 72, and Spanish lesson 5.7 by Friday. You will have a test in Spanish on Thursday, and during the week I want you to read *A Raisin in the Sun*." Then I look over at their assignment book to see they have it all there, as well as a plan for how to reach those end-week goals. Where do I get all this great filler for their books? Keep reading.

LIFE PLANNER

Just as with all meaningful life lessons for our kids, modeling is key. It does little good for me to tell my kids to wash their hands before emptying the dishwasher if I don't do the same. Beyond the principle of modeling, I would quite simply feel behind the 8-ball most of the year without my planner.

First, a disclaimer: I have lots of friends with beautiful planners that are handmade with pen-and-ink sketches of their week and beautiful quotes they have copied with calligraphy script and watercolor grocery menus for the month. I am not that girl. I think their planners are inspiring and gorgeous— and daunting, if I am honest with myself. If I had to pull that off weekly, I'd be a puddle. But, if that is your sweet spot and you have the time, by all means invest in beautiful organization.

TEACHER IN SERVICE DAY

Back to the puddle. Sometime in early August, after I have ordered curriculum for the year (which I map out in May while my brain is in school mode and buy as I find it on eBay or through sales by August), I set aside a day to plan.

This is a special time just for me.

I ask my husband to get all the kids out of the house for the afternoon or maybe even the whole day. It's not that I need all that time to work on my planner, it's just that I need all that time. Catch my drift? I am preparing myself for the year, too. I am taking time to dream big about what the year could hold. I am reflecting about what I loved about our previous year and what I dislike going into the coming year. I am thinking through various ideas to make the coming year even better, and maybe sitting down with a good book for an hour to inspire me.

Our kids grow up every year and our system must constantly be reevaluated and often modified to meet their changing needs. This is another reason why I want my curriculum plans out of the way—this is not about assignments and daily details but the big picture. And in the process of planning, if I discover that I want to try something different with a subject, I can return it or resell it. Rarely in this process have I needed to change curriculum (that awareness typically pops up mid-year, if at all).

I call it "Teacher In Service" day, which makes it sounds official and important so the kids come home impressed with me, but truly it is such a delight to dream and plan for the year; I look forward to it every summer. Below are questions you can use to guide your time.

ASK YOURSELF

- What is something I would like to do with the kids this year that would help me enjoy them as the gift that they are?
- What is a character theme that would benefit our family this year?
- What makes me feel lucky to homeschool this year?
- Where can I challenge my kids to try harder?
- How can I raise expectations of my kids to take on more for themselves and work myself out of a job?
- Where do we need to slow things down, backtrack, and revisit a subject or life skill or love lesson?
- What am I not looking forward to about teaching this year?
- Which of our systems might need to be tweaked now that our kids have aged another grade?
- What is something I want to leave my children as a legacy—an experience, skill, or belief—that I can work into our year?

You will notice from these questions that most of them are big-picture questions. "Life Planner" really sounds grand, doesn't it? We all know we can't really plan life; we just prepare for our best guess and welcome change with flexibility and patience as we meet it. That said, I prefer to "plan" our life from a month-per-page perspective. It is more practical to plan, more adaptable to change, simpler to keep track of, and, quite frankly, an easier way to dream.

FROM DREAMING TO PLANNING

After I did some dreaming one year, this is what I mapped out for my planner:

Teacher Assignment

TOP 3 GOALS	BEST THINGS ABOUT THIS MONTH	CW:	C:
		SCI:	SONG:
		MEM:	TOUR:
		NOTES:	

TO DO	SUN	MON	TUES	WED	THU	FRI	SAT

First off, I chose a monthly planner with big margins so that in the upper-right corner I could easily chart for each month across the whole school year in a short amount of time. Described in the following section are the categories I charted out in August in the top-right corner of all my pages for our September through June school year.

Not all categories were offered each month, and if one category required a large amount of time in a month I placed it in a month with fewer holidays and would lighten the other subject loads around it. Also, for our household of four kids, it was easier in some subjects to address a topic collectively and then adjust assignments up or down to fit the level of each child.

• **CW:** Each month I picked a Creative Writing focus for us. This category included: how to take notes, how to write a poem, how to plot a story, how to write a picture book, and how to write a short story. So, the upper corner for October reads CW: poems, and for November reads CW: note-taking, and so on.

Expert Tip

Do you know that many public libraries offer a service to teachers to collect books on a unit in advance for them to use with their class? And do you know that service is often extended to homeschoolers? This was a major boon for me when I met Sheila, the community librarian in our children's services department, and she offered this to me for free. After planning out my year in August, I reached out to Sheila with a list of 10 months and each science subject beside that month, what grade range I wanted the materials, and what day of each month I wanted to pick them up. Sheila was amazing. The first Sunday of the month I would walk back to her office, dig through the pile she saved for me, and collect the resources that seemed like a good fit. Simple, easy, and thoroughly awesome. Sheila saved me hours upon hours of time every month, not to mention the stressful scramble of "Ack! The book I need isn't in stock!" and it made science easy at our house. Thank you, Sheila! It's worth checking if this service is available at your library. If not, team up with a group of parents so each of you can pick a science category, research titles, and then share the list. (Just make sure you pick different months from each other when it comes time to reserve books). If you want to extend science even further, chart out astronomical events for the year so you don't miss whatever comet is coming through next.

• **SCI:** For each month, depending on the season or experiences, I assigned a science topic. Examples included: DNA, moon/stars/light pollution, sea life/ocean preservation, bacteria/hygiene, winter weather/hypothermia/avalanche, storms/volcanoes/typhoons/monsoons, trash/recycling, organ anatomy, and cellular structures. For each of these, I collected a pile of books from the library (be sure to see the Expert Tip to the side) and then followed the kids' interests in the subject to YouTube videos or a project we could do together that month. Typically I picked a few books I could read aloud to all of them that month, and then some age-specific texts I could assign them during their individual reading that would either overlap with our group reading or extend it deeper/farther into the field.

• **SONGS:** In answer to the last big-picture question above, one year I realized I wanted to bring some of my childhood memories of singing with my dad into our homeschool routine. Dad and I would often sing hymns together (to this day, I still sing the tenor part in a higher octave) and I wanted to extend that legacy to my kids. So each month I map out one hymn for us to sign together at Morning Meeting. When I started doing this, I printed off the lyrics for them and thought it would require major teeth-pulling to get through the measures. Surprisingly, the kids loved it. Especially hymns with a chorus they could memorize quickly. I found them humming the tune at random times in our day, and it was uplifting to all of us. We have extended this to learn various songs from America's history (such as all the verses in the national anthem). Admittedly, I was stunned at the enthusiastic cheering of my kids the day I presented them with a stack of hymnals, a gift of one for each child—the same 1960's edition that I used with my dad. (Go, eBay!) They are now following along with the notes and practicing sight reading alongside the words. Candidly, we probably include it in our meeting three times a week. But by the end of the month, the kids know the hymn for that month by heart. Whatever your background, perhaps there are songs, words of wisdom, poems, or other meaningful works that resonate with you; I encourage you to include these in your time together.

• **MEM:** Each month we memorize something together. It is easier than it sounds. If I simply read it aloud at Morning Meeting each day and leave it on the table propped in the center for them to read on their own over snacks or meals, they typically have it memorized by the end of the month. Kids are such sponges! And it beats memorizing the back of the cereal box. Examples of what we have memorized are: the Gettysburg Address, poems by Shel

Silverstein, famous sayings or Psalms, the preamble to the Constitution, and Roosevelt's *Citizenship in a Republic.*

• **TOUR:** Field trips are fabulous. No matter where you live, there is something to see. I grew up in a former logging town in southern Oregon, and one of our highlights was visiting the plywood plant to see how plywood was made. Even as an adult, I can still smell the fresh cut wood and resin in my memory. If you can join a field trip co-op to share the organizational burden (more on co-ops and groups in Chapter 4), that is a great use of team muscle. If not, set aside some time to plan a few tours a year. One year our co-op organized field trips with the theme "how life works" and we saw behind the scenes at the fire station, dump, post office, grocery store, hamburger chain, library, and pizza place. After each visit I had the kids write (or dictate) a brief summary of their trip and printed it out with a photo from the trip for their End of Year Binders to maximize the learning opportunity. (We cover EOY Binders in Chapter 10). We also wrote a thank-you note as a group (often with original art by the kids) to show our appreciation to our hosts and to model gratitude for our students. Just because I have this category written on the top of each month doesn't mean we have to go on a tour … it just keeps me on the lookout for the opportunity.

> Make time to celebrate your work —not just for the value of the work itself but for the value of the person doing it.

• **C:** This stands for "Consider" and is a flexible category each month where, if I feel like we need to school outside the box or we are blasting through our work, we can be superstars and extend ourselves into something new and fun. We definitely don't get to it every month, but the months when we do I am grateful for the gentle shoulder tap reminding me to Think Big. Ideas have included: learning the ukulele, experimenting with the Barchowsky handwriting method, learning five new recipes they can make alone, decorating a cake, logic and deduction, reading comprehension tricks, word roots, sewing/mending, art movements (Impressionism, Realism, etc.), watercolor painting, sketching, journaling, major artists (Dale Chihuly was a hit), and pottery.

• **NOTES:** This is also a good space for big reminders. In September, I list "adjust to new normal" in this category as a reminder to myself to move daily with intentionality and patience, since there is always a little friction as we transition from summer. I might jot a reminder to myself for October, "girls ready for Rosetta Stone?" or in February, "Evelyn: start cursive?" so I can reevaluate based on how they are managing their core subjects if it's the right time to add more. It may seem obvious, but sometimes the school year just disappears from under our sneakers when we hit the ground running in the fall, so these reminders are a big help.

• **BEST THINGS ABOUT THIS MONTH:** On the left corner of the page are two helps that are less about homeschooling and more about supporting the teacher. Just as it is important to reflect on areas of need or struggle, it is also critical—maybe even more so—to reflect on success. Admittedly, when I get my head down in work mode, I forget to pause and celebrate. So in August, I write this empty heading at the top of each page with three bullet points, to push myself to look back on the month and celebrate a few wins before I flip the page. This comes in especially handy on "brown days," as Dr. Seuss called them, "when I feel brown and low, low down," like I live in a circus of chaos and spilled oatmeal and juvenile property disputes. I can quickly look back and lift my eyes to the bigger picture. It helps. One of the challenges with being a homeschool teacher is that there are no promotions. There are no raises or accolades or positive feedback sessions, as other careers have. It is important that we make time to celebrate our work—not just for the value of the work itself but for the value of the person doing it.

• **TOP 3 GOALS:** Also key is managing expectations of myself. As much as I would like to be Wonder Woman, I am not. (Oh, for those golden cuffs!) Because the to-do list grows like the serpent heads of Hydra, I try to pick three goals each month and put them in the top left corner for me to address. While I likely won't know all my goals for the year in August, I can at least make a box for them on each page at the start of the year to remind me to focus on a few top priorities when I turn to a new page each month. And even though my list of jobs rattles tirelessly down the left column of my planner, if I can cross off even two of the three big dogs for the month, I feel like I have accomplished something. (Confession: There was one month when I forgot to list my top three goals; at the end of the month, I picked the three biggest needs I had met and put them in the box so I could cross them off. It still felt great.)

This planner strategy works because our literature/history/geography curriculum comes with a lesson plan so I don't have to build our own units. If you aim for DIY units, you may need a larger planner with more space for charting curriculum plans.)

On the other hand, if you are using pre-made lesson plans, those beautiful teacher planners with ample space for assignments may make it difficult to keep the big picture in mind. For example, there is no need for me to write all four of my kids' math assignments in my planner—that's just busy work for me. I am not the one doing the math pages, they are. We all have our own planners and assignment books and we all practice using them.

My "Teacher In Service" day is also the time when I schedule our grading periods. It's a simple exercise, marking "progress report due" and "report card due" twice each into the calendar, taking into account holidays and time off from school. There is no rigid rule in homeschooling that says the grading periods must be an equal number of weeks apart, or that grades are due in a certain month; adapt them to your calendar as it makes sense for you. But write them down, or you might do what I did one year and get all the way to December before realizing you missed two report card cycles. (Stay tuned, we cover a whole lesson on grades and report cards in Chapter 10.)

One last caveat on the planning: Aim high. If you aim at nothing, you will hit it every time.[1] I'd rather set my bar at "attainable but ambitious" and end up accomplishing slightly less than I hoped for than to set my bar at "doable but mediocre" and miss the opportunity for us to grow.

HOW I USE MY PLANNER

There are many practical ways I have used my planner to balance our lives.

Before a new month begins, I flip the page and fill in major dates—not appointments, but my husband's work travel schedule, special events, holidays, and birthdays—anything that might impact our school morning or require us to anticipate and make extra space in our lives. If we are a part of a co-op that year, I put that into the routine as well, since that will influence our school times and I need to counterbalance our work around it. (I learned early on that it isn't possible to do our standard homeschool workload on a co-op day—it's just too much.) By focusing the planner on life events that impact school or are relevant to school in some way, it simplifies my perspective as the teacher and makes planning school each week a lot easier.

In a section above, I outlined how to plan for the year and dream big in August. Once the year starts rolling, I flip over a new page to those big dreams and see if I need to track anything down to make them happen—recipes, a ukulele, a dissection kit, you never know. It's best to have it all lined up in advance so you don't lose precious weeks tracking down the materials. And, speaking of materials, once I come back from the library on Sunday with my pile of science books, I can put down the start dates for the science titles alongside our literature read-alouds so I can pace our reading time accurately for the month.

Because the planner is such a central part of our routine, we have made it the drop box for our classroom. Whenever my kids finish a test or paper, they "turn it in" by placing it in the front page of my planner. It's one less organizational box to have sitting on my counter picking up dust, and it keeps me accountable to grading quickly so I can get their pages out of my space and back into their hands.

> Aim high. If you aim at nothing, you will hit it every time.

On the inside flap of my planner is a list of notes with easy solves if I feel stumped under categories of: Lunch Ideas, What's For Dinner, Solo Work (listed by child, if I need to send a kiddo off on his own for quiet work time). I also have a section labeled "Bucket List" for all those great ideas I get from friends during the year; because it is not dovetailed into my monthly sketches, this often becomes a resource for the following year since I don't think to check it regularly.

In the back of my planner (just because there isn't space in the front) I have a Brain Dump Section for "Ideas to Try," "What's Not Working," and "Fun Family Ideas," so, again, I can capture all those light bulb moments in one place instead of hunting for lost sticky notes later. This page is a great place to start the following August when I reflect and plan for the next school year.

Finally, I have a page for "Funny Things Kids Say." Since we are together all day, they are always coming up with something so hilarious I think I will never forget it but do, so I write it down.

WEEKLY OVERVIEW

In my book *Study Smart, Study Less*, I introduced a tool that has had such a significant impact on all my students that I want to include it here as well: the Weekly Overview. Originally, something I developed for myself in college to track my weekly course schedule and manage "dead time" efficiently, I went on to use it with my high school students and then later adapted it to use with my first grader. It is usable and effective for that entire age range, which is pretty incredible.

Weekly Overview

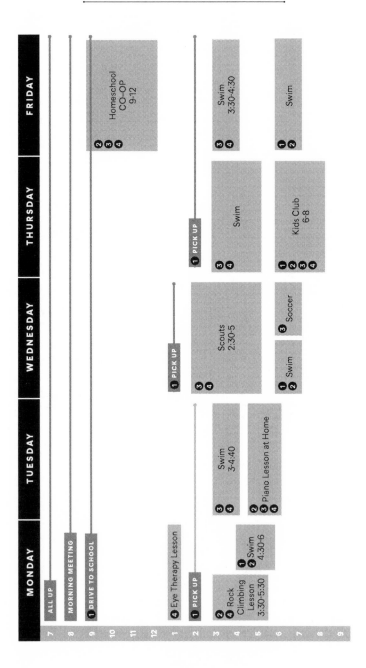

What is it? The Weekly Overview is simply an empty chart for a whole week with time slots from morning to night. This tool is for observing patterns and pockets of time, not for scheduling. (It's something we build for our family at the beginning of each semester or sports season so everyone can see where time is being spread or bottlenecked and we can adjust as needed.)

I initially attempted the Weekly Overview with my first grader out of a moment of frustration. (Frustration, I think, is more often the mother of invention than necessity.) Our first grader was angry. He saw that the younger siblings did less work and had more play time than he did, and he was convinced that his life was full of woe and work and that between a few basic subjects and cleaning his room he would never see his Legos again. There were tears. There was fury. So I pulled out tissues, markers, and a Weekly Overview. Together, we drew in all the boxes of how much time it took him to do math (15 minutes, but I let him say 20), reading (same), cleaning his room (20 minutes, but I let him go with 30) and whatever else he could think of in his daily routine. We filled in evening boxes for his once-a-week club and soccer practice, meals, and any regular family commitments. What was the end result? You guessed it: Just a few skinny stripes of color and inches upon inches of wide open white space.

> Frustration, I think, is more often the mother of invention than necessity.

His expression and body language changed instantly. He looked up at me with a tear-stained face and beaming smile and giggled as he realized the ridiculousness of his storm. "All that could be Lego time," I said, "if you are able to get your schoolwork done quickly instead of dragging it out. You win or lose by the way you choose.[2] So what do you choose?"

That young man is now a high school student. The other day I peeked over at his list of assignments and obligations that would overwhelm any freshman only to see pencil marks down the side tallying how many minutes it would take him to complete each job—something he had done himself to minimize stress and maintain efficiency. While not a Weekly Overview, he had adapted the concept to what he needed— I was proud of him.

So, outline a Weekly Overview, grab some markers and your kiddo, and see what you can make. This is a great tool to help your students visualize time— which is a difficult concept to grasp when 5 minutes and 50 minutes can sound like the same thing. It's also a helpful tool to design as a family to see where some days are busier so you can intentionally block other days for catching your breath.

Time Ladder

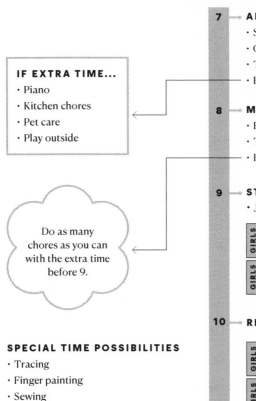

7 ➛ **ALARM!**
- Shower/dressed
- Clothes in hamper
- Tidy floors/counter
- Breakfast & vitamins

IF EXTRA TIME...
- Piano
- Kitchen chores
- Pet care
- Play outside

8 ➛ **MORNING MEETING**
- Bring assignment book & chore list
- Talk schedules
- Heart Talk

Do as many chores as you can with the extra time before 9.

9 ➛ **START SCHOOL (YAY!)**
- Journal first–prep your mind

GIRLS		BOYS	
Handwriting Spelling		Math	
Math		Handwriting Spelling	

10 ➛ **RECESS: OUTSIDE FOR 20 MIN**

GIRLS		BOYS	
Language		Chinese Typing	
Spanish Typing		Language	

SPECIAL TIME POSSIBILITIES
- Tracing
- Finger painting
- Sewing
- Video game
- Board games with Mom
- Baking! (Ooh... fudge...)
- Tea party
- Facetime with grandparents
- Dance party–you get to DJ!
- Build a fort together outside
- Paint toenails
- Work on photo journaling project
- Origami–look up new designs!

11 ➛ **ART & LITERATURE: MOM READS**
- Bring quiet art
- Science
- History
- Geography

12 ➛ **LUNCH: AIM TO BE DONE!**
- Clean up

1 ➛ **SPECIAL TIME!**
(If you finished school by lunch)

TIME LADDER

Oh, man, another chart? Yes. Trust me, once you get these in place, your school days will be so much easier. The Time Ladder[3] is one of my absolute favorite tools because expectations and needs are super clear and as a result our children learn how to manage time for themselves. It saves me a whole lot of headache having to play sheriff and chase them down.

The purpose of the Weekly Overview is to chart out one *week's* standard time commitments with the aim of discovering free or clogged pockets of space in the schedule in order to adjust accordingly. We build it once a semester. By contrast, the purpose of a Time Ladder is to design a plan of your ideal class *day*.

The Time Ladder is what I like to call a Flexible Structure. It clearly identifies goals for the day while also outlining them in a format that is adaptable to the alterations that inevitably come. The Time Ladder helps my students see at a glance what is expected in the pattern of our days and then work their way down the list to the bottom.

The idea is to build a dependable, attainable routine and post it where the kids can see it. If your kids feel like doing math before language, or language before math, that's up to you—flexibility can be a beautiful thing, especially when our kids *want* to do their schoolwork. Please keep in mind, however, that some students who struggle with anxiety or executive functioning challenges may do better following the same order of subjects every day.

Blocking out time with clear expectations enables everyone to get their work done. If the breakfast dishes aren't done by 9:45 or the puppy pees on the rug or grammar takes longer than normal, it does not throw off our schedule—we just keep working down the ladder. Structure without rigidity; it's a beautiful thing. We use it daily.

What works for my family may not work identically for yours. Your time is not my time; your kids are not my kids. Test your own versions of a dependable, attainable routine that works for you, your children, and your work schedule.

While both the Weekly Overview and Time Ladder are useful in their own right, the Time Ladder is particularly useful for helping students with varying needs and gifts prime for work each day. So if you are working with students who experience anxiety disorders or executive functioning challenges (or even if you aren't!), absolutely include all these visual structures in your routine.

HOW MUCH TIME DOES SCHOOL TAKE?

The general plan is this: Aim to work on math, reading, and writing five days a week for 15 to 20 minutes each subject. Then aim to work on science and history two to three days a week for 15 to 20 minutes. Please note, these times are just an estimate. In the beginning, when your student is adapting to your new role as teacher, a math lesson may take 40 minutes that later in the year might take less than half that. There is definitely an adjustment period.

I mentioned this in Chapter 2 but it bears repeating here: Once you have transitioned into your new routine, school at home will take less time than it does in a traditional classroom because the ratio is 1:1 or even 4:1 instead of 30:1. For homeschoolers, it typically takes about two to four hours a day to school an elementary student, four to six hours to school a junior higher, and five to seven hours to school a high school student at home, with no extra homework.

THE POWER OF THE VISUAL SCHEDULE

Have you ever told your 6-year-old at breakfast that he has a dentist appointment at 2:00 that afternoon, and then 5 minutes before you need to leave he is standing by the door ready to go with no prompting from you?

Neither have I.

In my early homeschooling years, my life looked a lot more like telling and retelling (and then correcting) my ducklings about which direction we were headed and what time and then the flurry of *Why didn't anyone remember!?!* Why relive my mistakes?

In one of our therapy sessions, Sam's coach asked me to create a way of showing (rather than telling) what was going to happen during the day so Sam could prime mentally and physically to get ready ahead of schedule. After a few iterations, we landed on a large laminated poster with Velcro tabs next to times of day running down the left hand side—a visual schedule.

The night before, I would attach little laminated strips to the Velcro that were color-coded for where/who and then an icon/words for the what for the whole day. (No, you aren't crazy and neither is our layout designer...there are no icons shown on the sample Visual Schedule on the next page because at this scale the icons would look like blobs. You will just have to take our word for it, or get your own set free with the video series to see for yourself.) For example, green meant home, orange meant away, yellow meant visitors. I had a smiley stick figure next to "friends" on orange paper showing we were going to play with friends somewhere else, and the same icon/word on yellow paper to show friends were coming over to our house. Whether it was a repairman, free play, or meals, everything had a colored tab. It took almost ten hours to locate the right icons and wording and develop drafts into a usable printout, and 5-10 minutes to arrange each evening for the next day. It was worth every minute for how much it helped Sam de-stress and prepare. (The printouts for the Visual Schedule are available online for free with *Homeschool Like an Expert: Video Series, Lesson 1.*)

What came as a surprise was the positive impact of the schedule on my other three children.

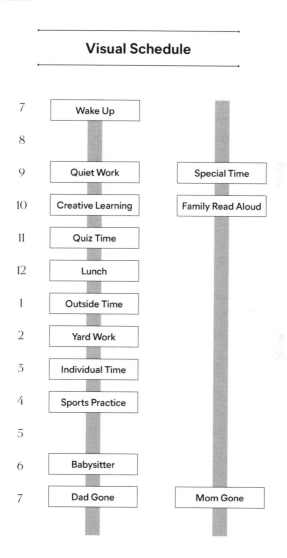

Within a few days of using the final version of our new Visual Schedule, I discovered I was doing a lot less reminding, and answering fewer repeat questions about where and who and when. In almost no time, the kids showed a preference for checking the chart over asking me. Using a visual schedule trained my kids from an early age to be ready ahead of time so we weren't running around searching for missing soccer cleats when it was time to leave for practice. This prevented a lot of stress for all of us.

I especially loved how the kids could glance at the visual schedule from the breakfast table and see at a glance based on colors whether they had large pockets of free time in their day or an afternoon of errands—and they could plan on their own. (It had a similar calming affect as the Weekly Overview did for my son the day he realized he had more time to play that he thought.)

> Whatever your family's core values, I encourage you to build that into the heart of your day at the start of your day.

Those were all wins, but best of all was how the chart became my wingman. If a child came to me upset that he isn't allowed to ride his bike after dinner because he has to finish work inside, I could take him to the chart and ask questions about where he spent his time during each of our blocks. When the tab said, "School," was he doing schoolwork with us or hiding? When the tab said, "Tidy Time" was he cleaning his messes throughout the house or playing in his room? The chart was clearly there, and if he clearly didn't use it then it clearly wasn't something he could be mad at me about. (Clearly.)

HAPPY MONDAY!

We continued to use the Visual Schedule until my youngest reached a first grade reading level, then graduated to what we fondly call the "Happy Monday! Board." It's a simple, inexpensive letter-sized whiteboard and at the top each day I write "Happy ___day."

Before Morning Meeting, I write out the plan for the day and set it beside the Time Ladder. Remember, the Time Ladder shows the general plan for how to work through school, chores, and piano practice on a daily basis; that doesn't change. Whereas the Happy Monday board shows specific events for the day, so it might read:

- 7:30 Morning Meeting
- 8 Start School w/Mom
- 12 Lunch

- 1 Read w/Mom
- 2:30 Leave for dentist
  - › Evelyn to soccer
  - › Evangeline to rock climbing
  - › Boys to swim practice
- 6 Home for dinner

As you can see, this is not a place to chart out subjects, just how we are blocking time for the day. It's super easy and fast to jot down, it accomplishes similar goals to our velcro Visual Schedule (as well as the same payoffs) and brings our team together daily to make logistics doable from the start.

MORNING MEETING

By now you've heard me reference this mysterious practice quite a few times. At Morning Meeting my kids show up to the table dressed, fed, and ready to go at the same time every school day. It is a guaranteed time for us to meet together before the day gets rolling, not only to go over logistics, but to dig into something deeper about life. When they show up dressed, fed, and ready on time they earn dessert with dinner, which has been an easy natural consequence to get them to the table each morning. And if I forget, I guarantee the siblings keep track and keep me informed.

After logistics we spend time on group holistic education, which is a fancy way of saying we talk about the stuff in life that matters to us most. This is a great place in the day to incorporate your family's faith and culture in your daily routine, to talk about current events, or to do a character study and develop cultural awareness over the issues that are most important to you. Whatever your family's core values, I encourage you to build that into the heart of your day at the start of your day.

At the end of Morning Meeting we have "ready, break" where I assign each of the kids a 5-minute job as a chore break. Those kids with someplace to go that afternoon will also set their supplies by the door before coming back to the table with their school baskets.

YOU WANT ME TO DO WHAT?

My mom almost never gives me parenting advice unless I ask for it—not that I don't need it or want it, but she's respectful to wait to be invited into that space. I'm grateful for her sensitivity and hope I will do that well someday. That said, there have been a couple times when she has made simple observations that were like a loving 2-by-4.

One such time was after she had spent the day with us when my eldest was 3 years old. We had gone for walks and played and eaten lunch and had all kinds of fun. After watching my conversations with my son and all the back-and-forth of a budding scientist about why we don't throw food, lick sewer grates, or dry our hands before using soap when washing them, my mom said simply, "Wow, there sure are a lot of steps to doing a job right."

I thought about that. Then I did some adding. Just to wash hands my son needed to do 10 steps in this exact order to get it right. If that was the only thing he needed to learn all day, I am confident he would get it right. But there were so many more subjects for him to master: table etiquette, going potty, street safety, riding a bike, using manners, putting on shoes—and they were all multistep jobs. No wonder he scrambled their orders from time to time! (And no wonder I was so tired!) He was a bright little boy and eager to learn and please—but there is always a learning curve.

> I soon learned that either I direct our attention toward something positive while in the car or it would disintegrate into slug bug and seat wars.

Where is this story going?

Easy. If you find yourself with a kiddo who struggles with the order of tasks at any age—anything from those preschool lessons above to your son struggling to remember all of his supplies for basketball practice each week—write up a list, laminate it, and tack it in a visible spot where he can manage it himself. Use what you know about your child's learning preferences to make life easier.

For our kids, we took photos of them doing the job when they were little and pasted their own little clip art into the steps—they loved it (and were much more likely to look at themselves doing the job right). I even made a photo series reminding my sons of all the steps for hand washing—it worked like a champ. And since we posted it in our bathroom, many guests remarked that they had no idea how many steps it took to finish the job right. Glad to know I wasn't the only one.

Maria Montessori taught that we should not do for our children what they can do for themselves. Presenting basic instructions in a step-by-step way has given my children a sense of autonomy in everything from getting ready in the morning to cleaning a bathroom thoroughly. If you have given visual guidelines through the elementary school years, by junior high your kids should be well past that phase (and they will likely have learned a bit about logic and process along the way).

CARSCHOOLING

It's the joke that isn't really that funny among homeschoolers. If you live in a city where you spend more than 30 minutes a day on the road, this is a section worth heeding. When we lived in the Bay Area and Seattle, some days I could tally up hours of driving without trying—it seemed like everything was 30 minutes from something else. As is true of the Second Law of Thermodynamics, I soon learned that either I direct our attention toward something positive while in the car or it would disintegrate into slug bug and seat wars.

So I used car time to my advantage. I figured, *"Here is my captive audience,"* and that what I might not be able to get them to pay attention to at home because it was on the dry side was now a fascinating alternative to staring out the window. Even if they didn't want to watch the science film, they couldn't help but hear and absorb it. (We don't do headphones when we are together as a general principle— we consider it socially isolating.) Of course, for families getting around by tube, bus, or subway, using travel time to learn via headphones can be a great idea.

If we are memorizing a famous speech or poem together, I will record it on my phone and play it on a loop a few times while we drive so we can prac-tice. Of all the car-friendly learning options, my favorite by far has been our audiobooks. We have paused the books and had so many great car discussions inspired by our "reading" together that might not have been possible with all the distractions at home. We always choose books that are safe for ears of all ages when listening together, but I'm not concerned if the youngest doesn't understand everything happening in the plot; we fill her in as we go and she absorbs more than she even realizes.

Many public libraries now offer digital content for free, so it is fast to upload an audiobook to any smartphone and play it on the go. Remember those "dream big questions" we talked about at the beginning of this chapter? One of my desires that came from that brainstorming was to share great books with my kids that we could experience together and from which we could laugh and learn. Audiobooks have made that possible. Whether in the car or at home, it has added a lot of flexibility to our reading schedule to plug and play a book. Beyond that (compliments of the library) we have used science and math DVDs, immer-sion language tapes, assorted music in different languages, and biographical audiobooks while getting from A to B.

PHEW

If there were prizes for reader stamina and long chapters, you would win it. Me too. I am awarding myself a DQ Peanut Buster Parfait for this one. I hope these tools support your teaching and bring you joy at work as they have me.

---

¹ Thanks, Zig Ziglar.

² Thanks, *Antshillvania.*

³ While I wish I could take credit for the concept of a Time Ladder, I got the idea from Benjamin Franklin. Now, there's a guy that got a lot done in a day.

8

How Do I Find the Best Curriculum?

Navigating Curriculum Choices

M
any parents new to homeschooling begin by asking, "What is the best curriculum?" when really the question they should be asking is, "What is the curriculum that best fits my child's learning preferences, my teaching philosophy, and our family's needs?"

Yes, the second series of questions is a mouthful, but it's the right way to go about this process. And there is a reason I saved this topic until midway through the book, even though it is one of the first questions most parents ask. As we have discussed in the previous chapters, there is so much more to learning than books. (So if you skipped ahead to this chapter, go back!) It is easier to figure out what curriculum is best for your child once you have first outlined your daily schedule needs, your child's learning preferences, and your plans for building a homeschool support system.

(In addition, your decision to homeschool privately or publicly, or to pursue public or private school at home makes a difference in this lesson—all four methods are unique, as we discussed in Chapter 2, and will affect how you choose curriculum.)

What is curriculum? That term has been commonly used elsewhere to mean a series of courses, a syllabus, resources, or information. Used in this book, "curriculum" means a series of lessons, assessment, and other content taught in a specific course. Basically, a math book, science quizzes, spelling tests, and history videos all qualify as a curriculum.

There is an ocean of curricula available for purchase, and sometimes that can feel overwhelming. As tempting as it may be to spend enough for a good used car on learning supplies, it doesn't take all that. In fact, it's a lot like when your child was an infant and you walked into a megastore feeling like you needed one of everything, when you came to discover later that you really didn't.

Based on what you know about your child's learning preferences, this chapter digs further into finding, selecting, and testing the best curriculum to suit your child's needs while keeping your family's time and budget in mind. It also addresses strategic ways to seek out curriculum, as well as ethical, inexpensive work-arounds to spend less on homeschooling while still getting great materials to suit your children's needs. Even if needs change mid-year, there are creative ways to adapt. Finally, this chapter discusses where to access curriculum affordably, and how to get the most out of your investment. This is a behemoth of a chapter, and if I can quote Mark Twain, "I didn't have time to write a short letter, so I wrote a long one instead."

THE UNICORN MYTH

Before we go any further, let me dispel the greatest myth that exists about curriculum: That there's a single perfect option. I call this the "Unicorn Myth." Too often, parents doubt their curriculum choice, feeling like, *If I could only switch to a different math program, math would be easier.* Sometimes that inkling is correct and a switch is the right decision—we will talk about that part way through this chapter. But for now, assume that there are mediocre to marvelous choices out there, and that how your child responds to a curriculum is less about how much you paid for it and more about how you adapt it to meet your child's learning preferences.

HOW TO SELECT

In Chapter 6, you read about how to identify, support, and teach to your child's learning preferences. That discovery process becomes important here as we consider how to select the best curriculum based on how adaptable it is to your child's learning preferences. For example, if your child is a Kinesthetic learner, consider incorporating math manipulatives or purchasing a curriculum that offers a hands-on approach. (*Manipulatives*, as we mentioned earlier, is just a teacher term for something your child uses to learn by handling, such as counting with beans or blocks.)

Most curricula will work for Visual learners, and Auditory learners can often easily adapt by reading instructions aloud or by accessing some of the literature through audiobooks instead of printed ones. (Remember, having a learning preference does not mean that your child can *only* learn using his preferred mode, it just means that mode will make the content more accessible. In fact, the more modes your child uses, research shows, the better her brain will learn the material.)

Next, consider content, method, and delivery—and which will be the best fit for your family.

CONTENT

Content seems straightforward—if you want your daughter to learn math, you buy her a math book. Yes, but just because she was in seventh grade last year does not mean she needs an eighth grade math book this year, especially if you are switching to a new curriculum.

Ridiculous as it sounds, there is a significant variation from one curriculum to the next in defining appropriate subject material for certain grade levels. On one occasion, we tested two math curricula in the same year for my son, and even though both were rated at fifth grade they were almost three grade levels apart in terms of content. I know of one student who transitioned from a private school in eighth grade to a public high school as a freshman, and even though the private school used an arguably more rigorous curriculum, the student had a few significant gaps in math by transitioning between two companies.

> How your child responds to a curriculum is less about how much you paid for it and more about how you adapt it to meet your child's learning preferences.

On another occasion, I took a different child all the way through sixth grade math and, out of habit, stopped by the curriculum fair that summer for my annual perusal of books before ordering. As I flipped through what would be his seventh grade math text in the exact same product line as his sixth grade book, I became confused. "I am sure I am missing something," I said to the salesman, "but isn't this the same content I just taught my son in your sixth grade math book?" "Yes," he acknowledged, "it is the same content. We have found that many families pull their students out of school for junior high, and the students are often behind in some of their math fundamentals, so we readdress the same math in seventh grade that we did in sixth because most parents don't want to drop down a level in math even though that's probably the right thing to do. If your son got As in his sixth grade math book, just move him up to the eight grade math book—he will be ready for it."

The eighth grade math book was a perfect fit. So inspect the table of contents and as many sample pages as possible before purchasing. If you are unsure what your student learned prior to homeschooling, invite him into the conversation so you can look at different grade levels together and find the best fit.

METHOD

Method is about your approach to learning together. Here are a few questions to get your thoughts percolating (and please do not feel pressured to answer any of them right now):

- How much time are you able to devote to homeschooling each day, especially if you have a family business or both parents work outside the home?
- Do you have any special family considerations that may make your homeschool world look different from the norm, such as a spouse who travels for great lengths of time, a child with unique learning needs, significant budget constraints, or an unusual work schedule?
- Do you think you want to be more hands-on in your teaching approach (doing every problem together with your student, for example) or do you prefer more of a coaching role (getting her started on the subject and letting her work through it on her own)?
- Do you like the structure of textbooks, or would you prefer to develop your own unit by bringing together multiple resources? (Developing your own unit, by the way, is an advanced level thing to do—if you do it at all—so please feel zero pressure from this question. Very few families build their own homeschool units since there are now so many great companies that do the work for us.)

All these methodology questions will influence what curriculum is the best fit for you.

If you are working full-time while educating your child, you might want to start out with a curriculum that doesn't require you to instruct directly, such as a digital program or online course. Estimating how much time you have to teach, based on your family's needs, is a great place to start when looking for a curriculum that is the best fit.

Delivery is how you prefer to access your content. Some families choose to take courses online, either as an individual program a student progresses through at her own speed or as a member of an online classroom. For parent teachers looking to outsource the grading of the work through an online class or a self-grading computer program, this can also be a good option. Both reassign the instruction to a different teacher, which may be important for parents who are working or who may not feel capable of teaching that subject. Some families select video courses so they can watch the content together, giving the parent some quick subject review and instructional help and keeping parent and student on the same page.

Other families have concerns about screen time and prefer the more traditional delivery of textbooks, which may or may not be built with independent learning in mind.

> Wait to purchase your five core subjects until you have identified all five, since some curriculum companies combine subjects.

Another approach to delivery is the "one room schoolhouse" model, where all siblings study the same content together with assignments modified for whomever is at the table. Sometimes this can be a great approach for families with multiple siblings clustered somewhat close in age--I have been able to do this with history/geography/literature/science with children spanning four grade levels.

Whatever delivery method fits your situation best is up to you. Remember, homeschooling will not look like traditional schooling, so be willing to think outside of the box when considering delivery. The goal is to select whatever will help your student learn best given your time and resources.

NARROWING YOUR OPTIONS

Sometimes, the easiest place to start in your search is with fewer choices. Here are a few ways to consider simplifying your search:

CORE SUBJECTS

When shopping for curriculum, begin with your core subjects—math, reading, and writing. Once you have located those, expand to science and history. To the extent it is possible, I encourage you to wait to purchase your five core subjects until you have identified all five, since some curriculum companies combine subjects and you may discover materials with a dovetailed approach.

If this is your first year homeschooling, I recommend waiting to invest in any other content areas until you have tried out your five core subjects for a few months to see if you need to make adjustments.

More is not better. In fact, sometimes, more subjects is worse because it requires more time, focus, and juggling on the part of student and teacher. As tempting as it might be to purchase yearlong courses in personal finance, photography, Latin, engineering, mixed-medium painting, survival skills, logic, and robotics, go easy on the electives—especially if you are new to homeschooling. If there is an elective truly speaking to you, try to limit yourself to adopting one per year at first, and let it drift in and out of your weeks so that it does not come at a cost to your core subjects.

> "Classroom privilege" often applies to schools that have paid an additional fee for the privilege of photocopying for additional students.

If, as a family, your students are so diverse that you cannot possibly pick a singular elective to discover together, wait until each student is mature enough to safely manage the tools and basic learning to discover his elective subjects on his own with you in the wings.

Until that time, look for ways to open up avenues of creativity that don't require curriculum. For example, our daughter loves problem solving and design, and shows a natural aptitude for engineering. Until she had the maturity and focus to use some of the more dangerous tools needed, we developed a "tinker box" for her as a gift—a plastic organizer bin full of spools of thread, wire, clips, brads, buttons, bells, toothpicks, duct tape, pipe cleaners, and all kinds of toggles and baubles she could use to turn into something creative. The best part was that she could play with the box on her own during the afternoons without supervision. So even though I would have loved to add engineering to her core, it was better for her to explore on her own with library books and a tinker box so that she was able to stay focused on math and reading in that season.

Going back to core curriculum, notice that some subjects (or brands) require more time each week than others—and that may be what you want. Or you might need to overinvest time in one subject and pull back a little in others while you transition into homeschooling to get your student up to speed in a certain subject area.

In balancing timing, be sure to save time for life outdoors. As we discussed earlier in the book, there is an inherent value to incorporating play into our days so that our children have the opportunity to invent, create, and collaborate with friends. The goal is not to cram as much content into their day as possible now that we can feed them concentrated doses at home. We need to be just as intentional about creating spaces in the week for our students to explore their city, build forts with friends, visit museums with a buddy, or rescue a baby bird.

COPYRIGHT ETHICS

As you look at various curriculum companies, I encourage you to ask whether or not you are allowed to reproduce pages for multiple children. Some companies have built their curricula with family flexibility in mind; others will not allow it. I realize it is tempting to photocopy an entire workbook to use with all your children under the "classroom privilege" exemption, or to forward materials to your friends that you have paid for online and downloaded because it is "school related," but that's not how that exemption works. Classroom privilege often applies to schools that have paid an additional fee for the privilege of photocopying for additional students. Copying materials without having paid that additional fee undermines the very company whose material you value. So if the ability to photocopy ethically is important to you, look for that as a feature in the materials.

SIBLINGS

Finally, when deciding how to select the best curriculum, keep siblings in mind if you have more than one child. Some of the curriculum I have purchased over the years has been more expensive initially, but since it is non-consumable (meaning, it doesn't ever need to be marked, cut, or written in) I have been able to use it with all four children ethically and adapt it to their learning needs, making it more affordable over time.

WHERE TO FIND CURRICULUM
HOMESCHOOL NETWORK

One reason why I strongly encourage parents to locate an online homeschool network before beginning to search for teaching materials is that, oftentimes, a network of expert homeschool parents can be a great place to start.

If I am seeking out a rigorous math curriculum for middle school, the first place I might turn for information is to my experienced online homeschool community. I will either contact parents whose teaching practices I respect, or toss out the question to all on the list to get a sense of what other families are using. After listening to advice and looking further online, if the publisher does not list a substantial number of sample pages, I will reach back out to those parents and ask if they would be willing to let me either borrow the book or send me pictures of the table of contents and a handful of pages. From there, I will look at various options with my student to see what she finds engaging or makes sense to her. It's also helpful to be able to ask parents directly for feedback on the curriculum.

KEEPING CALM AT THE CURRICULUM FAIR

Prior to the internet, one of the original methods for homeschoolers to locate textbooks was a curriculum fair. Many fairs are still offered around the U.S., though honestly it is not the first place I send new homeschoolers simply because it can be overwhelming. The best way to make use of a curriculum fair as someone new to educating at home is to visit the fair's website simply for the vendor list, and use that as a starting point in your online search.

If you decide to attend a curriculum fair so you can hold material in hand before making a decision, I encourage you to enter the building with a short list of what you are considering in order to focus your search. Aim to solve the cores of math, literature, and writing first. Oftentimes, solving those first three may lead you into curriculum for handwriting, spelling, science, and history. But, start with the first three subjects and do your best to wander through the fair looking only at those three to begin.

For those who don't live near a fair, this same method applies to sitting down at the computer: Write up your list. Start with the core three subjects. And try *not* to go down the tempting rabbit holes of other subjects until you know more about your core.

At the fair, avoid making quick purchases; browse for an hour or two before buying. Over the years I have made many core decisions--but *very few major core purchases*--at curriculum fairs, even though many companies offer discounts. Instead, I'd purchase resources at the fair that would be difficult to locate online. Anecdotally, the curricula I have been most happy with over the years were from companies that did not pressure or upsell me at a fair but encouraged me to go home and think about it. Before buying a new brand of textbook, I often try to borrow it from friends to gauge my kids' reactions, shop for used resources through our homeschool network or eBay, and purchase online when I'm ready.

While many curriculum fairs can be expensive to visit, others may be free or have a reduced rate if you just want access to the exhibit hall. Some fairs offer reduced or free entrance to first time homeschoolers, but you typically need to request that ticket online in advance. Many fairs need volunteers and will trade one entrance ticket for a certain number of hours worked. So don't let the entrance price keep you from going if you feel compelled to visit.

At the beginning of our homeschool journey, I chose a rigorous math curriculum and, before buying it, borrowed a copy to show my kids. They begged me to pick something else. The pages were in monochrome and they said it didn't look fun. So I borrowed an equally rigorous math book from a different publisher that had colorful lollipops next to long division problems. They said that was the book they wanted.

It's worth asking your children for preferences sometimes between two strong contenders you are considering. However, please don't expect your kids to pick what curriculum will best suit their needs. I have known some parents that let their kids shop through the fair on their own to decide what core subjects they wanted to learn that year, when really that's our job as the teacher. In fact, if you are able to leave your kids at home during the fair that will probably be your best case scenario.

Curriculum Search Resource

As you wander through the fair, ask lots of questions. The folks at the booths would likely welcome a conversation. If you are genuinely interested in their product, ask if you can take a couple pictures of the cover and a few inner pages so you have an easy reference when you get home. I am a Kinesthetic learner and it helps to get my hands on the page and to talk with someone about it in person.

HERE ARE SOME QUESTIONS TO ASK:

1. Are the number of words on the page appropriate, challenging, boring, or over-whelming for the reading level of my student? Is it adaptable to my child's needs?
2. Is the monochrome or colorful page design helpful, boring, or distracting?
3. Is the teacher's role flexible or required? Does it encourage the autonomous student or require us to work together full-time, and which teaching philosophy will be best for my student and for me?
4. How much prep and active time does this curriculum require of me as parent

teacher, and how does that fit with our family's lifestyle and my work schedule?

5. Is this the right level for my student? Just because it says eighth grade, does it mean this is the right level for *my* eighth grader?

6. Will this book intimidate or inspire my tender reader? If the former, is there a way to use the stretch to build a new character skill, or is this a battle not worth fighting (yet)?

7. Does the literature read like a snoozer (and feel like vitamins) or grab the reader from page 1 (like potato chips, where you can't read just one page)?

8. Is it adaptable to my child's learning preference, and can it be easily expanded to include siblings, either now or in the future?

9. Does it support our family values? If not, is there a way I can use it to open up a meaningful conversation with my student about different perspectives?

10. Is it consumable (such as a workbook that the student writes in)? Is that OK, or do I want to resell it when we are done? Is there an ethical way to work around the consumable part?

ONLINE

After having read the previous section about curriculum fairs, please do not feel like you need to attend one. Online is a great way to go. In fact, some math providers offer free placement tests online, and that is also a great way to decide on the appropriate level to buy. If your student is caught between two grades, consider starting with the easier grade and then accelerate your student as needed. This ensures you don't have gaps in your child's math foundation and makes learning a more positive experience to start.

CHARTER RESOURCE

For parents enrolled in public homeschooling through a charter system (please see Chapter 9), you can start with these first two steps and then reach out to the Teacher of Record at your charter for additional recommendations. Please remember that the state has a list of approved curricula; you can choose a program that's not on that list but won't be reimbursed for it.

TRADITIONAL ADAPTATIONS

For those parents schooling at home through an online academy, online public school, or a private online school, there may be adaptations or curriculum alternatives available to your student. For instance, a friend of mine growing up had Cystic Fibrosis, and as a result was regularly out of school. The school modified her lesson plans to include streamlined assignments, since she spent a great deal of her time in hospitals and recovery. If your circumstances or your student's needs require something different than the standard lesson plan or supplies while schooling at home, be sure to ask your school for modifications.

HOW TO TEST YOUR CURRICULUM

ADJUSTMENT PERIOD

After purchasing your curriculum, it's time to test it. First, recognize that in the first few months there may be an adjustment period when changing to a new curriculum. Terms, instructions, and layouts may look different from what you used before. And if you are beginning homeschooling, your child will also be adapting to your new role as parent teacher. Lower your expectations just a little in the beginning to give everyone time to adapt.

OBSERVE

Second, after the adjustment phase has passed, begin to observe how your child interfaces with the materials. Is she engaged? Regularly confused? Able to find answers on her own? Or completely lost without your help? Some of this is age dependent. By third grade, however, depending on your curriculum, it is reasonable to expect that your student is able to answer initial questions on her own.

MODIFY IF NEEDED

Third, if you sense that the curriculum is not meeting your student's needs, don't rush out to buy new material right away. Instead, do three things. First, go back to the preface or teacher's guide to see if there is something you missed. Second, check out the company's website or call their customer service department--often there are trained educators who can walk you through a way to use the material in a new way. Third, many popular curricula have fan sites where homeschoolers discuss new ways to use the materials, so throw your questions out there and see what comes back. Once you have taken all those steps, reconsider creative ways to adapt your curriculum to your child's learning preferences. (I offer a full chapter of creative ways to apply and learn new material based on learning preferences in my book *Study Smart, Study Less*.)

Ultimately, remember that you are in charge—especially if you are homeschooling privately. If your child has mastered a concept after the 12th problem and there are 20 more, there is no need to kill them past the normal drilling. ("Drill and kill" is what review is sometimes not-so-fondly called.) Curriculum companies are often generous in providing more problem sets than are needed so that teachers addressing students in different environments have a way to assign more or less. Please understand, review is a valuable way to maintain mastery, so I'm not suggesting you skip it entirely. But aim to find the balance. You're in charge.

WHEN TO SWITCH

Let yourself off the hook from the get-go and expect to switch curricula in some subjects at least once in your child's educational career. Making a switch is not a sign of failure to anticipate your child's needs; more likely, it is a sign that your child is honing his learning preferences and you are understanding his needs better.

Also remember that there is no magic unicorn when it comes to curriculum, but there are certainly reasons why a switch is in order. First, consider the possibility that the curriculum is the wrong pace for your student—either not rigorous enough to maintain her attention or so fast-paced that it is difficult for her to keep up. That is a great reason to change.

Second, it is a good reason to change if your student has not mastered the content before running out of material. One year, we ran into a wall with one of my children and math. We had a move, a new baby, and a surprise diagnosis all within six months, and somewhere along the way I dropped a stitch with him and his multiplication fundamentals. By the time I realized what had happened, we were a couple months too far into math and he was struggling. It was not my proudest moment as his teacher.

When life comes at us sideways and catches us off guard, we recalibrate. It wasn't his fault. I sat down with him, working back through the lost fundamentals to see where we could pick back up. But in doing that, it became clear that the idea of going backward through the math sections he had already completed was soul-crushing. I could respect that.

Rather than drag him back to Start like some miserable game of Sorry, I switched game boards and got him a different math book. I found a new provider that touted a different way of teaching math, and I explained he didn't have to do the whole book, only one section (which covered the buildup to the concept as well as the concept itself that he had misunderstood). It was a great compromise. It was not only a new page, but a new way of explaining the work.

He liked the new book so well that he continued with that curriculum for two more years until he asked to go back to the original. (On a related note: At that point it was clear there were gaps between the two curricula, so he had to do extra work to catch up. I explained this would be his last switch in math while he was homeschooled; he understood and was willing to put in the work.)

What do we learn from this long story? Switch with caution. Beyond that, there is the additional lesson that if you find yourself in a season where you can't teach at 100%, it's worth pausing or slowing some of the lesson plans so you don't create a new problem by forcefully moving ahead beyond what you can thoroughly teach. The win for me, even in my failure to catch the problem early, was in the beauty of a tailored education—seeing a need, making a switch, recovering, and moving forward. It didn't need to cost my son summer school or being held back a year—just a quick switch and some elbow grease, and he was good.

> Please do not push your student into the next unit if he has not yet mastered the former.

This is not an uncommon occurrence. At some point in all of our student careers, we have felt lost. The beauty of homeschooling is that we parent teachers are in the driver's seat when our students get stuck. Do we buy an exact replica of this textbook to have our student work over again? Do we buy a new brand? Do we make up our own? Do we use online supplements or apps to fill in the gaps? Do we just keep moving through the content and hope our student eventually figures it out?

While the answers to the other questions are up to you, the answer to the last question is a definite no. Please do not push your student into the next unit if he has not yet mastered the former. However you choose to get him back on track, this is another scenario when a curriculum change may make sense.

SWITCH CAUTIOUSLY

As we talk about scenarios for switching curriculum, I have a strong caution that has been handed down to me from the previous generation of expert homeschool parents that I value highly: Do not change curricula more than three times in a subject in your student's career.

That advice has especially held true for core subjects like science, math, and history. In fact, you saw it play out in the story above when my son switched back to his original math curriculum and had to catch up before he could continue.

The order in which material is presented can vary pretty significantly between one company and the next, and switching curricula often could lead to gaps in your child's knowledge base.

Of all the subject areas, math is perhaps the most difficult to change, so aim to start and stick with one curriculum company as much as possible—modifying and supplementing if needed—to create a consistency in learning. It can be incredibly disruptive to students to switch curriculum year after year just because parents find one they like better. Unless your child is struggling significantly in your current curriculum (and supplements won't help) try to stay put.

> Do not change curricula more than three times in a subject in your student's career.

In addition, if your student is struggling in a subject area, realize that the challenge may not be with the curriculum itself but with the structure of your homeschool schedule, teaching style, or environment. It's worth tweaking those first before going through the disruption and expense of switching materials. Consider going back to Chapter 7 or the Quick Start Guide for ideas of what you could modify outside of textbooks.

CURRICULUM BUNDLES

Now for the fun topic of bundles. Almost all newcomers to homeschooling love bundles. They feel safe. Parents are often drawn to the idea of getting everything in a box with premade lesson plans and educator videos. For many families, bundles are a great way to start homeschooling and ensure there are no gaps. They can be an especially good fit for parents who don't feel capable of fully addressing all the content on their own. If a bundled curriculum is what works best for your family, go for it. Just know in advance that even though it sounds like less work, it will still require the parent teacher to sort through the material, find ways to adapt it to their child's learning needs, and pare things back or supplement when needed. Remember: There is no teacher in box.

I suggest that you shop for bundles carefully. Some publishers advertise that purchasing theirs saves families from having to figure it out themselves because they just get one of everything and therefore will have all their bases covered. The challenge with this model is that, unless you are certain you want one of everything in the kit, you may end up paying for materials or books that go unused. Additionally, some new parent teachers end up feeling overwhelmed when it comes time to plan school at home for the week because there are way more pages and options than their student needs or is capable of completing.

Please understand, I am not trying to dissuade you from purchasing bundles; I think they are great and I buy them for some subjects. I am just encouraging you to shop carefully, especially if you are combining all your subjects into one box. Our family's math, spelling, penmanship, health, science, composition, and literature/history/geography are by six different publishers. It doesn't feel in the slightest bit scattered; it feels like we have what we need.

IF BUNDLES DON'T SEEM LIKE A GOOD FIT

For other families, bundling is not a good fit. To start, curriculum bundles can be expensive. Another challenge with buying a bundle is that you may end up losing some of the autonomy of homeschooling because you may feel locked into someone else's lesson plan. By the end of the year, some families find there are books left over that they paid for but never used because they ended up customizing the lesson plan more to their student's needs.

One creative solution is to purchase only the lesson plans from a company rather than their full bundle. Some curriculum companies will create a dovetailed lesson plan using outside resources that merge history with literature and geography, assigning writing tasks that cover all three. This sort of bundling allows families to adapt a lesson plan across multiple age ranges. It also provides flexibility so that parents are not required to purchase every book on the list but can source whichever books they choose from the library or used book sellers.

ANSWER KEYS AND LESSON PLANS

Your comfort level with the subject and available time will determine whether or not you want to purchase answer keys for tests and quizzes and/or lesson plans.

Sometimes keys are a huge time saver—especially for math, science, and grammar from grades three on up. An experienced homeschool mom gave me this advice years ago, and it has been gold for us: have my students grade some of their own work. She was right.

From third grade on up, I purchase answer keys for math, among other subjects. (In fact, part of my selection process for math has been the quality of the answer key. I don't just want the answer, I want it to show step by step how the problem was solved.) After teaching my student a math lesson, she will complete it and show me she has answered all the problems. At that point, I hand her a red pen and the answer key and she grades it while sitting near me.

By handing my child the answer key, I am inviting her to unlock the mystery of what she missed. For Sam, this grading style has been especially calming, focused, and helpful. From a practical perspective, it also makes grading a whole lot easier than all my kids handing me a stack of textbooks before lunch—*Have fun grading all that, Mom!* I needed a way to make grading doable in our day. If we aren't grading, we aren't learning. Students need to know what they are getting wrong so they can learn how to get it right. However, as I have said before: My students are not your students, so do what is right for you.

As for lesson plans, I have found them to be helpful in subjects that are either dovetailing curriculum or presenting content that is not my strongest area of knowledge. Many parent teachers struggle with science, and in this case the teacher planner could be hugely helpful if it provides a lot of background information to cover questions their students might ask. For some companies, lesson plans are optional; for others, they are not—so inquire before buying. Ultimately, my aim here is to free you up to purchase less--to realize there are some places where less is more and you really don't have to have one of everything.

CHEAP SOLUTIONS
THE TWOFER

One way to save money homeschooling if you have multiple children is to look for a curriculum that enables you to bridge multiple grades with a single book and adapt assignments. Why purchase and teach two kids two sets of curriculum when you can consolidate?

For science, literature, and art, I teach according to the spiral method. The spiral method exposes your student to a subject (such as physics) at least three separate times in her academic career. That would mean a year of physics in elementary school, a year (or semester) of it in junior high, and a year of it in high school. Repeated exposure to the topic breeds a sense of familiarity with the basic principles of physics from a young age, so that when she approaches the subject in its entirety as a high school student it doesn't feel completely foreign.

It is great to expose a first grader to physics, and totally OK for him to understand levers and pulleys but to space out at gravity. (Ha! Just making sure you are still awake...) By the time he meets up with physics again in high school, it won't be nearly so intimidating because he was exposed to it twice before. The twofer spiral method may not be available in all subjects (such as math) but science, literature, and history are good options. Not only can you save on curriculum, you can better balance your time. You can teach up or down a grade level to tailor the lessons at the right speed for your different students.

The twofer also creates a natural space to have your Bigs read library books to your Littles, since they are both studying the same subject. Not only will it meet any appetite your older child has for "playing teacher," it will serve as a good review of basic content for the older student, bonding time for the two of them, and a chance to develop your older child's oratory skills. For the younger student, being read to by an older sibling will likely make the subject even more attractive because it is something they do together.

BUY USED

Buying used curriculum, either online or through your homeschool co-op, is another great way to get excellent materials for less than the sticker price. Expert tip: Used curriculum tends to be cheapest in the spring and most expensive in the fall.

FREEBIES

Homeschool parents, many of whom are educating in a one-income household, are great at sharing. Chapter 4 talked about the value of co-ops, and resource sharing is a big part of it. It is not uncommon to see regular posts in our co-op for, "Does anyone have X book by X publisher I could borrow for a month?" and to see multiple replies of, "Yes." And many co-ops offer a regular "free table" so parents can leave gently used books, learning tools, clothes, toys, or infant items for anyone in the co-op who needs them. There are also great free curriculum resources available online--check our "Links to Experts" on HomeschoolExpert. com for a list of suggestions.

BUY IN BULK

Look for ways to buy school supplies in bulk. For example, it is much cheaper in the end to buy 1,000 loose sheets of paper through an online distributor than it is to buy a 50-sheet pack from the grocery. And with multiple kids, that adds up.

E-BOOKS

Sometimes saving money involves spending it. I am embarrassed to say that one year our family paid $95 in fines to the library. We call it "Year of the Garfield's." It was terrible. (And yes, the children in question helped pay the tab ... it was tough-love-painful.) After we licked our wounds and recovered, we looked into e-readers. We made a family plan to have our 9- and 11-year-olds work toward earning their own e-readers. It has become a rite of passage for our other two children to reach the age where they can earn theirs too.

Expert Tip: Stock Up on eBooks

For those new to eReaders, all libraries developing their digital bookshelves have a way of deleting access to the library book from your account once your time limit is up; if you want to renew it, that's up to you. This is great because it means no more late fees. However, it also means books are sometimes deleted before finished.

Ever looking for ways to beat the system, my 13 year old figured out how to max out his library card with digital books and then put it on airplane mode until he was done reading all of them so that the library couldn't delete them from his device. Technically, it was ethical—our local librarian agreed. They still deleted it from his account at the end of the time limit so other patrons could check out the book, and he didn't have to worry about renewing his books until he was done reading them and wanted a new batch.

We took this a step further one year when we were in the middle of a lot of transitions and moves by purchasing all our literature, history, and geography books electronically so we didn't have to schlep a giant crate of books around everywhere we went. (This turned out to have the added benefit of longevity—now I don't have a stack of dog-eared paperbacks to pass down to the next round of kids.).

Oh, and one more thing we love about e-books: I used my daughter's e-reader to trick her into reading longer books. True story. (Maybe I should label that "Confession" instead ...) One day I changed the setting on her device so she couldn't see how many pages were left to read, and then loaded up some library books that would have terrified her if she saw their length. She was ready, she just didn't know she was ready (and the size of the book would have prevented her from trying). I read aloud the first chapter to get her hooked on the story and left her with the e-reader to finish on her own. She flew through it. The best part was when I reserved the same book from the library and put it in her hands, "This is what you just read," I explained. She beamed. She was stunned into giggles. She felt huge. Sometimes parents have to get a little sneaky ... er, creative.

My last bit of e-book wisdom is classics. Publishers have recently been dumping volumes of great classic books online super cheap in mega-packs. We bought 25 Tom Swift books for 99 cents and 65 Arthur Conan Doyle books for the same price. It's hard to beat 90 books for $2 and no extra shelf space. E-books have made reading affordable and easy for our family. And as much as I am a Luddite who adores paper, I'm thrilled to see my kids excited about reading.

Now that I have charged on cheerfully about e-books, it would be right to add that there is reason to be cautious about the negative effects of screen time on melatonin and serotonin levels, especially on our children's developing brains. Scientists are still studying the effects of lit screens on neurology (and I do not claim to have expert knowledge in this area). I encourage you to shop for e-readers that are not backlit but have lighting around the front of the frame (if any lighting at all) to minimize the screen's effect.

CREATIVE SOLVES

Finally, look for ways to get creative with friends. Consider renting, borrowing, or sharing the cost of non-consumables with another family in your co-op. If you co-purchase it together, you can co-sell it together. It's common practice on homeschool chats to see parents asking to borrow a resource or teacher key for a short period of time, and families are often eager to help.

HAND HIM A SHOVEL

All children learn in phases. Some have more focus initially until rounds of hormones begin to hit, and with them increased stress and the sense that learning has become complicated. For others, the Hulk hormones of smash/roar/ crash are on high for a few years and school requires a softer onramp. Of course, some are Aesop's Tortoises, steadily working all the way through. This becomes an even greater challenge when your children are on different phases from each other at the same time (you may as well plan on that).

Be patient with them—and yourself. For every parent who has told me their child is an "early reader" I have met a parent with a "delayed reader." My mother was one of those parents. Books and family read-aloud times were a big part of our growing up years, but even with that she ended up with a 4-year-old reading at a second grade level and an 8-year-old who couldn't read "duck."

Mom liked to say that one of my brothers had a "thick" phase, when the best thing to do was to hand him a shovel and send him outside for a year or two to explore and play until his mind was ready to work. We had a lot of shovels and an acre of dirt to explore; it was marvelous. Eventually, that boy came back inside and discovered he liked reading well enough to read all the way through a university degree. Maybe you should put "shovel" on your curriculum list, just in case.

Ultimately, the key to developing bright students in our children is not curriculum. It is to foster a love for learning from a young age, encourage curiosity, develop integrity and compassion for others, and to show them they are loved. With that foundation in place, your curriculum will strengthen the wonderful adult your student is already becoming.

What is the Difference Between Public and Private Homeschooling?

Expert Help on Four Ways to Homeschool

W hether or not taxpayers have children enrolled in their local public schools, their tax dollars go to those schools. Free education for all is part of what makes America distinct. As a result of paying taxes, local residents are encouraged to take advantage of community resources their tax dollars support—and that includes both homeschoolers and the public school system.

For those new to homeschooling, it may be helpful to know that for some families, this is a sensitive topic. Chapter 5 lends insight into why some families feel strongly one way or the other about public (i.e., state-sponsored) homeschooling. That said, many families have adopted Public Homeschooling because they say they otherwise could not have effectively taught their children at home.

In returning to our earlier conversation in Chapter Two, it's important to reiterate the differences here, that Public Homeschooling is a slightly more malleable form of public school because it is located in the student's home, is directed by the parent and district, and is partially funded by the state. So cost is shared, autonomy is shared, authority is low. By distinction, Private Homeschooling, is the most customizable of all the forms of schooling, and is the traditional form of homeschooling that sought official legalization in the 1980's. This form of schooling provides families with the greatest amount of autonomy, empowering them to customize their curriculum and school schedule as it best fits their needs. That means cost is moderate to high, autonomy is high, and authority is high.

To address some of the practical implications of state funding and home-schooling, I have invited Bryn Johnson to join me for this chapter. As well as being a veteran homeschool mom and former professional educator, Bryn has been a Teacher of Record in California and Oregon for the past eight years in charter schools. (A Teacher of Record is someone employed by the state as a bridge between the homeschooling parent and the state to administer direction, support, and accountability.)

ANNE: Thanks so much, Bryn, for making time to talk with me today about your experiences homeschooling as well as maneuvering community resources in the local school district.

BRYN: You're so welcome, Anne. I'm happy to help.

ANNE: Could you give readers a little more background about who you are so they can have a better understanding of your perspective?

BRYN: Sure! I have experienced education from many sides of the table. I am a teacher by training; I taught for three years at a private school; then I left my career to homeschool my two daughters for 10 years. In those 10 years we used private co-ops, Classical Conversations [a homeschool program], and charters at varying levels to supplement our homeschool life all the way through—some of which I directed. Unfortunately, when we moved to Oregon, there were no charter schools available in our district, at least none I could find. We had enrolled in a charter where we lived previously in California and liked it.

As a mom who schooled at home without a second income, charter schools gave me good support in figuring out how to transition formal teaching methods to homeschooling, and made a way for us to afford to give our kids quality curriculum and extracurriculars. Because of our charter school, I knew I could get help and that we could afford to give our kids access to lessons in piano, art, and ballet—I was grateful. Eventually, we found a charter here—or maybe it found me—and I ended up getting a job officially as a Teacher of Record, continuing to homeschool my daughters at the same time. I feel like we have run the gamut of all the different sides of homeschooling and teaching, especially now that I teach in a public charter school.

I have been homeschooling since my first child was a kindergartner. I felt like we were home too much and I thought maybe she was too isolated during the day, so I enrolled her in kindergarten halfway through the year. That only lasted a month. It was a terrible experience for both of us but I'm grateful for it because it helped me solidify why we needed to homeschool, and that she really wasn't missing out on anything. It became clear to me that what we were doing at home was good for her.

When I enrolled her in kindergarten, she was a really advanced student— she was reading early chapter books while her peer classmates were still learning basic letter sounds—so the school put her in a third grade class for her reading times. But when she got there, she felt very shy about participating because the other students were so much older, and the teacher chastised her for not being more involved—she was scared. Kids bullied her on the playground from both classes, she got physically pushed around quite a few times, and she even got head lice. Add to that, I was hauling our younger child around for school shuttles and messing up her nap times because the school bus didn't pick up where we lived, and I felt like we were all suffering. It just wasn't worth it, so I pulled her out to homeschool her.

From there, I made a bigger effort to arrange park dates with other homeschool families and we joined a weekly co-op, which helped a ton. Our two girls are 18 months apart, so as they began to age that also made things easier both from a social/friends perspective and also academically. I was able to teach their science and history together, and that made my job as parent teacher easier as well. When the girls reached eighth grade we put them in private school for a year and then have transitioned our oldest into public school this past fall; they are doing great. They are really enjoying learning with friends and have a solid education background going in—it has been pretty smooth. I really enjoyed having my girls home when they were little, establishing a solid foundation with their learning and being together—it really was a time I am very thankful we had together. But now that they are older, it is clear they need more.

While I am sure I could track down higher level math and science coursework for them through homeschooling resources, they really want to have the full high school experience: clubs, dances, team sports, various programs and electives we wouldn't have at home. They are excited about going to high school, which helped us make the decision.

ANNE: Could you help give me an overview of what charter homeschooling looks like, where new homeschoolers can access it, and why parents choose to homeschool through a public charter? (I realize the word "charter" has different meanings in different states.)

BRYN: A charter school in our state is a public school. I would say maybe 90% of the people I speak with in any context don't know that, including the ones asking to register, so it's something we have to clear up pretty frequently. It is a public school, it's just a different format from a traditional public school because it is done at home. Some states even call it "Public School at Home." Where I'm from, it's called "Charter School," but there are different names in different states.

[Anne: Some states use the term Charter Schools for a form of education that has nothing to do with homeschooling—instead, it's an alternative school that meets in a traditional building five days a week. It's unfortunate that the names are the same, because that adds to the layers of confusion for parents looking for new education models. So, if you are looking into Public Homeschooling models in your state, do your best to clarify with a description as well as a title what it is that you are hoping to find.]

> When you sign up for a charter school you are no longer a private homeschooler, you are a public schooler learning at home.

That's the number one thing we need people to understand, because when you sign up for a charter school you are no longer a private homeschooler, you are a public schooler learning at home. There are some big differences in that wording.

The format of our school is a hybrid, and that's the beauty of it—it's my tax dollars at work for me. I am paying taxes while doing all this work teaching my children on my own with some choices, but I still have access to those tax dollars in the form of a Teacher of Record who is assigned to me from my district. Some charters service the whole state so it's important to know where your charter is based and what sets it apart from others, because all charters have their own unique flavor.

In Oregon, there are three ways to be schooled at home. (With COVID-19, there were four, but I will just talk about the traditional three.) First, you can take online courses through your local school district as a full-time public school student in your district sitting at your home computer. Second, you can school at home through a state charter program. You are enrolled in a charter, which is a public program that's different from your public school and that has implications I will explain later. Third, you can make a declaration to your school district in whatever format your state requires to say you are privately homeschooling.

In Oregon, the Educational Service District (ESD) requests state test scores in third, fifth, and eighth grades be sent to the local office. They do not control specific curriculum or scheduling beyond that. In some cases, homeschoolers may access public school resources such as band, orchestra, art, sports teams, or education therapy resources as well. Contacting your local ESD is important, as the services available differ widely between districts and states.

The charter we used most recently was based in a school district two hours away from us. Many families in our city also enrolled in this charter, which requires the two districts to communicate about funding and student coverage. Again, this varies from state to state: California had a rule that you can only enroll in a charter in your county or a county contiguous to yours.

ANNE: I had no idea your charter school was out of town. How do you participate in classes or social functions, or follow up with your Teacher of Record given that it is so far away?

BRYN: We have a set of Teachers of Record (whom I will just refer to as "Teachers" from here on out) at a campus in the city where the charter is officially located, and students who live in close proximity to that center can attend there. We also have satellite centers in neighboring towns where we rent buildings and students have the option of attending additional classes. Some satellite centers find creative ways to meet together in local coffee shops if there isn't an official building in every city. As a result, there is a little less contact for us than if we lived in the host city for our charter, but it still works.

For those who live in the host city, oftentimes the charter there will be more directive about which curriculum to choose for math or science so that it dovetails with other homeschoolers in that charter, enabling the host charter to offer classes they can take together. The flexibility of curriculum choice really depends on each individual charter and can vary. There are pros and cons to having more charter-directed curriculum versus a wide range of choices; it depends what you are looking for in your homeschool experience.

ANNE: So, why do parents typically choose to homeschool through a charter? What seems to be the driving force that draws them to the public versus private homeschool model?

BRYN: There seem to be a couple different crowds. One is families pulling out of the public school (or who are at the age to start public school) and have decided to homeschool but have no idea where to begin. Often, those families tell me they feel overwhelmed, lost, or are struggling to make homeschooling work and we want to provide support for them. This is where charters really shine because they can come alongside a family who otherwise might not feel capable of homeschooling to help make sure they are covering all the bases with a rigorous curriculum and not missing something basic.

The second crowd we tend to see is people who have homeschooled for a while and are actually quite capable of teaching their children at home, but it's an economic sacrifice or hardship. Their family is likely existing on one income and every bit of financial help matters—especially when it means being able to afford violin lessons or karate to provide their child with a well-rounded education in ways couldn't afford to do otherwise. We still provide the same accountability, structure, and support for that family with all the monthly meetings and such, but it is worth it to them to give up that time because they feel like the financial help makes a big difference in expanding their child's educational experience.

ANNE: So where should parents start if they are weighing their options between private homeschooling and public school at home?

BRYN: The starting point if you are interested in public school at home is to contact your ESD (Education Service District) and ask about first steps, whether you are transitioning out of public school or have a child just entering school age. If you are transferring out of your local school district, it's often required to send an email or letter to your district notifying them of where you are going and that you aren't in-district anymore, so there is a paper trail and accountability. Since there is funding attached to which students attend what districts, it's important for the district to know where your child's allotment is supposed to go and to take you off of their roster for truancy purposes. And once you are officially established with your charter, you meet with your Teacher to create a plan and outline expectations for the school year.

By contrast, if you decide to homeschool privately, you simply notify your district using whatever format your state requires and that's it; you do your thing from there. The allotment for your child will still go to the district where your child would have attended public school, and that is the district whose resources you may be able to access should you desire to later. Again, every school and district varies, so check with your local schools.

Each charter has different requirements and expectations for attendance. There will be some kind of daily attendance, typically checking in over email that you are home doing school. For instance, as a Teacher of Record, I not only check attendance, I also need to see families face to face at the learning center once or twice a month. At that meeting we check in, see how the schooling is going at home, the parents show me sample work with progress or proof of completion to ensure they are on track with their educational plan, and I ask younger students to read some sample material aloud to me or show me a fun project they are working on to verify schooling. Families are also welcome to come to campus for additional classes if they like, which are optional.

Our charter has kids who are totally virtual—100% of their classes are online. Our charter has some kids who take a few classes online and use textbooks for the rest. No matter the material the parents choose to use, the students can come into the centers anytime to take additional classes. Some centers or charters will offer more elective-type classes—like art or drama—while others offer core classes. It really depends, which is a great thing to ask about the various charters in your area if you decide to look into it as a possibility. Our area decided to offer electives instead of core classes largely because that resulted in greater attendance—the kids really wanted to come together with peers to take fun classes they were less likely to study at home. However, many families are looking for a math or writing class, and those are provided as well.

> It definitely gets harder to pick your own curriculum as you get to high school with a charter model.

ANNE: It sounds like curriculum choices vary from charter to charter. What should parents be aware of regarding benefits versus limitations of coursework selection if they choose to go with a charter homeschool program?

BRYN: As far as coursework selection goes, if it meets state standards, it is fine to use it. If you want to use something faith based for your curriculum that meets state standards, that may also be fine depending on the state, but the state won't pay for it. The curriculum needs to meet approved standards, and students will be required to take standardized school, district, and state tests to show learning. Also, students are assessed and graded and report cards are sent home, just like in a brick-and-mortar school.

This is different for high school, where requirements are harder to line up, so the charters typically hold fast to their list of textbooks or online programs and parents choose from there. For those families who do choose alternative curriculum, they have to prove proficiency by taking tests throughout the course of the program to prove knowledge of concept, which gets a little harder as not all math or science curriculums cover topics in the same order, so you might get a test out of order from what you are learning. It's tricky. So if your high schooler wanted to learn from a textbook of your choice for science, that might be possible—but then your student will have to take regular proficiency tests on pace with the other students learning from a standardized program or curriculum. It definitely gets harder to pick your own curriculum as you get to high school with a charter model.

Each family in our charter gets a $1,000 stipend per child (that figure varies from charter to charter) that is intended to go toward curriculum purchases if that student plans to use something other than the online curriculum our public school offers. They cannot use that money to buy a faith-based curriculum or a curriculum not on the approved list; it would be up to the family to purchase that separately. Any leftover money not used to purchase curriculum would then go toward extracurriculars. As a family, you would sit down with your Teacher before the year starts and discuss what curriculum you are hoping to use, and we would make sure each of the subject areas have their standards met with the scope and sequencing of the program you are choosing. The Teacher would then suggest alternatives to fill in the gaps if there are any.

ANNE: If parents considering homeschooling want to know what charters are available in their area, how should they find them? Is it through the school district or is there a nexus of information somewhere?

BRYN: To my knowledge, there isn't a central location at this time. Googling "charter schools in ___ state" would be the best place to start your search. Even if you find only one charter, contact them and ask your questions; also ask them for information about other charters in the area and they may be able to direct you.

It's important to note that the school district may or may not be able to direct you to charters in your area. Even though charters operate as a public school within the home, they are different from your local public schools. It's not that your local administrative school office doesn't *want* to tell you about charters, they just might not *know* because they are completely separate.

ANNE: Are there any limitations to homeschooling through a public charter beyond what we have discussed already?

BRYN: Families should come into the charter setup knowing there will be much less flexibility in regard to time, and that faith-based curriculum choices won't be covered. The accountability we offer can be both a pro and a con, depending on the family and what people want.

Some families really want that accountability to help them keep going or help them when they are frustrated or feeling lost or their kids are struggling. It's really a big help to families in that situation. For those who know what they are doing already, from that second group we just talked about, they might chafe a little under the requirements—especially if their timelines don't match up with the charters.

One of the big reasons families decide to homeschool is because of the flexibility and taking advantage of travel or life experiences during off-peak seasons, and it is difficult to do that through a charter. At times the deadlines and attendance feel a bit like a tug-of-war, where families are not completely free to do as they like in terms of scheduling; there are limitations.

Some say those boundaries are an interference and are almost offended to have an outside Teacher "up in my business." Families need to know there is a cost to enrolling in public school at home, that they must give up some of their freedoms to do so. You have to conform more to the traditional school schedule.

I had a family in the past who wanted to travel internationally, living and studying the culture for more than a month with their kids—super great life experience. But they had to take their schoolwork with them because they were still technically enrolled in public school at home. So for the first half of each day, their kids did schoolwork and in the afternoons they went exploring.

> Families need to know there is a cost to enrolling in public school at home, that they must give up some of their freedoms to do so.

ANNE: What are good questions new homeschoolers should ask their Teacher of Record or ESD before deciding public versus private?

BRYN: Here are some good questions to ask:

- How is your charter distinct from other charters, and what expectations and requirements do you have of the families enrolled in your charter?
- What types of classes do you offer at your base location, and are any of them required?
- What are the daily and monthly overall requirements and expectations in terms of paperwork, check-ins, and meetings?

- How do you handle attendance, is it once a week, twice a week, or daily? Is it something you do through email or text?
- What is your charter's method of being in school, and what is required as the parent teacher?
- How should I plan to communicate to you what I'm doing? Do you need a weekly lesson plan from me or a monthly plan or check-in?
- How do you measure student progress? What testing do you require?
- Is there any curriculum that is required to be a part of your charter, or is there a list I can choose from? If I want to use a curriculum that is not on that list, what is the process to get it approved?
- What if my child is falling behind, what can you offer to help me? Or what if my student is on an extreme end of the education spectrum, either very advanced or needing special educational support—how can you help support them and me?
- If I have a child with a learning disability or who needs speech therapy, what does your referral process look like and how do you support or monitor that?

My hope, of course, would be that the reason charter schools and parents collaborate is so we can individualize education plans for kids. We would ideally be able to customize what plan we make in each of those cases.

ANNE: What are some of the lesser-used resources that are available to homeschoolers through their districts? Can private homeschoolers access them too, or do they have to go through the public charter?

BRYN: As a private homeschooler you are able to access almost any service the school provides to a child within the district using taxpayer dollars. Not all homeschoolers know that. Speech therapy, sports, and music would be examples of things that may be available to you. This is one place where it is not as advantageous to be in a charter school, because many of those services are limited or restricted for charter school students.

As an example of this, one family who was considering enrolling in our charter had a student who was enrolled in the middle school orchestra in the local public school as a homeschool student. In the process of considering charter enrollment, they realized they would not be allowd to access orchestra any longer if they were part of our charter because their child would be dually enrolled at that point, and that's not possible. But as a private homeschooler, he could remain in the orchestra, so they stayed private.

This goes back to the two programs being in somewhat of a competition for allotment funds. There is wide variance to this, of course, state to state, and no way anyone could generalize about it accurately, so it's best to call your local district and your local charters to better understand how it works in your area. How this applies to sports or education therapies will also be determined by the district or state. There are some built-in reciprocities so charter students don't miss out on everything, but again, this will differ by location and state.

The general guideline seems to be that if there is a way for a charter student to use their curriculum funds to pay for an alternative group outside of the charter, such as a community orchestra, they must pay funds do so; but if there is no alternative football team they can join, they may be able to join the local public school's football team. It really isn't clear-cut, so I hesitate to mislead anyone here unintentionally, which is why I reiterate it is best to check with your local ESD. Typically, the ESD oversees the school district, which manages the school, which serves the individual families and homeschoolers—if that helps with understanding the hierarchy of decision making.

As a private homeschooler you are able to access almost any service the school provides to a child within the district using taxpayer dollars.

ANNE: Are state testing requirements (or grades) different for families who go through a public charter versus private homeschooling?

BRYN: Charter schools have exam periods, report cards, and grades just like public schools. If you are a private homeschooler, depending on the state, you may be required to take state exams during different years or sometimes every year and to turn those scores into the ESD.

A lot of people use Stanford-10 in our state for testing. Families in the charter school receive state testing for free each year; private homeschooling families pay for it and turn the results in to the district when it is required. Families are allowed to opt out of the state testing for religious or philosophical reasons oftentimes through their charter or private homeschooling, but we encourage them to take the tests because it is a helpful way to benchmark growth and maintain records.

ANNE: How do you determine grades for the report cards?

BRYN: Grades are determined by compiling a number of different sources, depending on the learning material used as well as the age of the student. For those enrolled in online work, I can see their scores daily. For those who are using more of a traditional curriculum for homeschooling such as textbooks, parents can track work and proctor tests and then bring these to our meetings to prove proficiency. To determine grades we use work samples, district tests, time spent in classes, monthly meetings, and conversations with the parents. It's a partnership.

ANNE: What are the downsides of joining a public charter versus private home-school? Perks?

BRYN: The one consistent complaint I hear from parents is that they want to work on a different timetable or schedule and take time off to do something outside of the classroom. Sometimes the parent has a change in a work schedule that makes a break possible, and at times we can work with that but oftentimes we can't—we are a public school, so it is tricky. This goes back to the traveling family I mentioned earlier who wanted to shift some of their work to summer and take a break mid-school year. They didn't take all of their school books with them, but they took a lot; they were immersed in the culture holistically every day, but they still had to do their math and turn in reports and assignments. You can't skip math for a month. If you want that kind of freedom, the public charter probably won't be a good fit for you. I think that's the biggest push and pull: the desire for complete freedom. We have that freedom as private homeschoolers, but not through public school at home.

> Charter schools have exam periods, report cards, and grades just like public schools.

As part of our grading cycle, students turn in work samples, physical education logs, and math updates at the end of every month. Some families turn in their updates a few days early, some on the due date, and some I have to remind. It's clear that some families really struggle to fit into our box. Over time I have learned that some families are very flexible in their learning style—their students are still learning, but deadlines are clearly not part of their organic learning environment. They are more like Unschoolers, and they struggle a lot to keep up with our requirements. They might not label themselves as Unschoolers but it's clear from their family culture and personality that they roll to their own set of rhythms and it doesn't really jive with our due dates. We are flexible where we can be, but definitely there are also some lines where we have to keep families accountable and we can't budge. So it's wise for families to take all this into consideration before joining a charter for the year.

On the perk side, beyond the curriculum stipend, the overarching benefit parents get is support from the Teacher, guidance on how to navigate their year, advice on what curriculums to choose, support for any kids who have special needs, and all kinds of special ed resources. Parents are not home alone trying to figure all this out. They have access to professionals who are trained and can help.

Overall, my closing thought is that I love the beauty of homeschooling, I love the freedom and the special times it allowed me to be with my kids, but I also liked having someone I could ask questions of or go to for support and that is why the charter option worked for me. I liked that accountability and liked checking all the boxes so I knew I wasn't missing anything, making sure my girls had a quality education. Charter schooling is a hybrid model between the two education types of private homeschool and public school, and for our family that really worked well.

ANNE: There is a definite pocket of homeschoolers that is concerned about participating in charters because they think that if the charter finds out their child has special needs, it will send social services in to monitor their work or may refuse to let them homeschool. Can you help address that concern?

BRYN: I'd be happy to. I should start by saying that what I am sharing is limited to my own experience—I cannot speak to what has happened in other states. But this is a common question I get, so I'm happy to go into it because I do think this is something that worries parents. Probably the best way to start is with a real-life example.

Let's say you have a student who is struggling to read. The parent has been consistent at home, the Teacher has worked individually or in small groups with the child, and still the child is struggling. This shows up in daily work, behavior, and standardized testing: This is a struggle that needs to be addressed.

At that point, the Teacher will strongly advise the parents to have the child evaluated for dyslexia and any other learning needs—if it turns out they have an actual learning disability, it opens up all kinds of new avenues of help and resources. With a diagnosis in hand, now we can get him access to special ed curriculum, specialized resources, or extra tutors. The Teacher will help that family access school resources that will lead to an Individualized Education Program (IEP) for their student, which could include assignment modifications, variety in showing competency, extra time allowed on work and assessments. Even their state exams and district evaluations may be modified according to their learning needs. So I feel like it's the opposite of what some parents might be afraid of—instead of their child struggling with no help in sight, now we can step in and provide help and have more accurate, realistic goals at each grade level.

Having an IEP helps move students forward. The same goes with speech therapy. Because my specific charter is a virtual charter school, the speech therapy for a family who needs it in our charter community will be delivered virtually because we are so far from our charter base. I have recommended to the parents to do both—to accept this therapy through the virtual charter and then to also seek out private therapy which, of course, they will need to pay for themselves, or insurance may be able to help as well. What resources they have access to depends on the school, the district, and the needs of the individual.

A parent came to me for help once because her adopted child arrived with a lot of learning needs, and she was overwhelmed. She felt like she couldn't negotiate everything on her own—at times the search for resources can be very confusing, even for parents enrolling their kids in public school. In some ways I feel like my role as her Teacher enables her to continue to homeschool because otherwise it might be too much for her to do alone. We are here to help parents help their kids.

To send social services to extract a child from a home because she has learning needs and is homeschooled is a myth. I have never heard of that happening because a child has learning disabilities or special needs. Speaking of society in general, I have heard of social services being sent because they suspect child abuse or a child not being fed, but that happens no matter what school a child attends—charter, private, or public.

I hear this one too: *What if my child can't pass the state test, are you going to take my child out of homeschooling and force me to put him in public school?* No, we're not. We're going to make a plan to try to help the family move forward if they are in a charter school. Even for private homeschoolers that is the case. The district will continue to collect and track those state test scores, and if there is a consistent failure to pass, the district will contact parents to talk through the benefits of getting tested for a learning disability with the aim of setting up an IEP. Parents often resist that, both in public school and in charters or private homeschooling, but it really does need to be recognized and honored if your child has a need that requires additional help. Ignoring it won't make it go away. That child can't go into high school not being able to read and write well, unless he has an IEP explaining why he can't read or write.

If parents resist help long enough and the child does not improve ... well, that's hard to say. It puts the Teacher in a really difficult position. I actually had a family withdraw from our program because I needed more accountability from them and wanted to create a plan to move forward with their child who seemed to be struggling, and they didn't want it. So they left the program. That's also something I always communicate to parents—you haven't signed in blood, and you can always withdraw, just as is the case with any public school. So now that mom is homeschooling privately and the accountability for her child's progress rests with her completely and the state will see that. The state won't likely monitor her differently. We are required to notify her home ESD that the family has returned to private homeschooling, and the state checks in with them on the standard testing years from there. I've never heard of a different reaction from the state.

> Some kids wouldn't graduate if not for charter schools working alongside them, and not every family situation will be great for homeschooling without support.

Now, I want to add here that parents of children with learning disabilities don't have to join a charter to access all of these resources—some are available to them through their school district as private homeschoolers. Either way, it is worth parents asking for help.

ANNE: There seem to be polarizing viewpoints on charter versus privatized homeschooling—an impression that choosing to receive money from the state has the potential to undermine homeschooling freedoms, and on the other side a feeling of rejection or disdain for those who elect to accept support from a charter. I suspect you have encountered this before. What is your response when you find yourself in one of those conversations?

BRYN: I feel like both perspectives need to be honored. I see the private side, and the fact that homeschooling *does* need to be protected. Even this year, there was a Homeschooling Summit [led by Elizabeth Bartholet at Harvard Law School] with the aim of doing away with homeschooling. That opposition is real, and I believe homeschooling is incredibly valuable and is a fundamental right that needs to be protected. I get that.

I also get the desire to do what is best for your family, and I honor and respect that.

But I also see the side that some people need help. Some people don't know what to do when their child is struggling to read, or they need more community, or they are not making it on one income and need some financial support, or they need ideas from an educational professional about how to tailor learning to their child. I see both sides. Parents should be able to make that choice for themselves.

When we need to fight for freedom, I am happy to do that. But I'm also thankful for the opportunity to use a charter as well and to support other parents who are schooling at home.

My perspective is generally limited to K–8. But think about a high school kid who maybe isn't doing well in school or maybe got pregnant or who wants to drop out. It's a reality in a lot of kids' lives. Why not provide an alternative for them, with a Teacher they can still access to ask questions so it isn't so daunting? Why not allow them to school at home with a charter to help keep them on track? Some kids wouldn't graduate if not for charter schools working alongside them, and not every family situation will be great for homeschooling without support. Sometimes having a Teacher of Record is necessary and helpful.

Sometimes we have seen parents who do not have a GED themselves trying to help their high schooler get an education and they want support. Or what about the mom who may not speak English as her first language and is struggling to teach her children at home?

The role of charters has, unfortunately, become a very emotional and at times derogatory conversation among homeschoolers rather than factual and objective, and I think we as a homeschool community need to do better at understanding the perspectives of those not living our lives.

Not every family looks the same. Not every parent can do what you have done in your home. And I think that is important to remember. I see the importance of being free and being able to teach your children as they need to be taught, so I am not advocating for charters for all. There are a lot of ways to get an education, and I think we should be flexible in that.

CLOSING THOUGHTS

As I said in the beginning, this is a sensitive topic for many. Those who have chosen public school at home sometimes feel excluded by those in the private homeschool community for electing to relinquish some of their homeschooling freedoms to the state in exchange for support. Conversely, private homeschoolers often experience financial hardship and sacrifice in order to safeguard homeschool rights by making a clear distinction between public education and private homeschooling; if their choice to homeschool privately is dismissed, they feel neither appreciated nor valued by those who chose to accept state funds.

It's best to approach conversations around this topic with compassion, restraint, and grace for each other. Let's assume the best of one another—that we are pursuing the educational path that seems to best fit the needs of our children and our families. And together, let's continue to pursue and protect the freedoms that were hard earned to make that choice.

10

Do I Need to Give Tests and Report Cards If I Am Homeschooling?

Using Assessment to Inform

I f you are new to homeschooling, you may be wondering how to determine if your child has mastered the content, or how grading and report cards work with teaching at home. Even if you have been homeschooling for years, there has not been much modeling historically about how to bring assessment to the kitchen table.

Children need feedback—both immediate and delayed. If we only give them immediate feedback, they struggle to see the big picture of their growth and become discouraged; if we only give them delayed feedback, goals seem unattainable. It takes both.

This is one of those lessons I wish someone had handed me at the beginning of my homeschool journey, and I am grateful to be able to share it with you after learning from experts for the past two decades. However, before we launch into the practicals, let's pause to look at the big picture.

THE BIG PICTURE

When homeschooling parents talk about grades, we tend to have two approaches. The first is that we think grades and report cards are not really relevant to homeschooling. That the traditional purpose of grades is for the school teacher to communicate with the parent about student progress, and since parent and teacher are now the same person, report cards are no longer necessary. Some homeschool parents also express concern that tests and grades are not only unnecessary but that they potentially stifle the love of learning and create stress. Unfortunately, this approach makes it difficult for students to measure progress and learn how to manage success and failure, which is a real life skill.

Another common approach is when we elevate grades and national percentiles to the highest level of importance. When we feel like A+s down the card get our child that much closer to a happy life and in some ways validates our role as teacher. Our family lived in Silicon Valley for many years and observed some parents spending a remarkable amount of time and resources training their children from a young age how to test well. I believe those parents wanted what was best for their children—to make sure their children had all the help they needed to succeed in life.

But at times, the desire to support our children can become a pressure on them to achieve, and even to become an extension of our own success. Achievement pressure is not a new concern. It has been well documented and has been a significant discussion in education communities for some time. Homeschool parents, unfortunately, are not immune to wanting our children to reflect well on our work as their parents and teachers.

I can certainly appreciate both views—the desire to encourage our students to excel and also to foster a love for learning. For parents transitioning into homeschool for the first time who are accustomed to report cards, this may be a new conversation for you. Perhaps you are already comfortable with traditional academic grading and are looking for a way to build healthy evaluation into your child's education at home. If so, read on.

A THIRD APPROACH

Taking all that into consideration, what if we adopt a third perspective of assessment? What if we saw grades and report cards as neither trophy nor disciplinary measure, but as a useful tool of measurement? What would it mean if we disconnected grades and report cards from performance baggage, both for students and parents? Report cards and exams would then become benchmarks—ways to measure progress, to make sure our children are learning, and to identify any areas where our children need support. We could use those benchmarks to help our children develop the life skill of setting healthy goals, managing achievement, and learning from failure.

Life is full of tests. In the real world we are always being graded or evaluated, promoted or demoted. It is important to teach our children resilience—how to aim high as well as how to recover emotionally if they miss the mark. And if we have older students preparing for college, it is crucial to expose them to report cards years in advance to help with that transition.

Every semester I give our children report cards that extend beyond letter grades to a holistic view of what they have learned and accomplished during that term. In addition to assigning letter grades for school subjects and character focus areas, I write a narrative that reflects on her character development, a recap of her extracurriculars, an overview of what we learned that semester, a section about her strengths, and a few bullet points listing areas for her to focus on during the next semester. Finally, I include a quote about what she wants to do with her future; for our older students, I insert some of their wisdom on life.

My students love their report cards. (Yes, that came as a surprise.) In fact, if I get delayed on completing their report cards, they ask about them. They are birthday-present-excited to see how their hard work has paid off over the last few months. Their excitement at getting report cards tells me we have struck a healthy balance.

For our family, report cards and grades are effective tools that make progress measurable. They help me communicate to my husband how each child is doing every quarter. And they bring our children individually into the conversation so we can coach them about setting goals and developing character and a healthy work ethic.

Report cards enable my children to measure their own growth and motivate themselves.

> What if we saw grades and report cards as neither trophy nor disciplinary measure, but as a useful tool of measurement?

Assessing our children through grades and report cards has enabled us to celebrate their progress and create space for a practical conversation about where to go next in their development. Grades are not a high pressure trial; they are an opportunity to grow.

So before you launch into grading your student, take a moment to decide what your purpose is: Is it to give measurable feedback, set goals, show room for growth, and celebrate it? Consider what positive message you can communicate to your child about grading. With all that in mind, let's lay out some practical tools.

REPORT CARDS

As we start with report cards, it is important to review an important point: Yours is not mine. Your report cards may not look like my report cards because your child is not my child. I will lay out what I have done for my family with the understanding that you will build what works for yours.

The goals you established for your child at the beginning of the school year (see Chapter 2 for guidance on setting three main types of goals) come back into play here as you think about evaluations. Reflect back on your bottom up, top down, and core family goals. Did your student learn what you wanted him to learn? If so, applaud where he succeeded, and provide specific support and guidance where you know he can still grow. Grades and goals work hand in hand, communicating where we have been, where we can improve, and where we are aiming.

> Using report cards to tell the story of our children's progress through the year (and years) blesses not only the student, it blesses the teacher.

NARRATIVES

If letter grades feel like more than you want to start with, consider using a check system instead as a warm-up. Report cards are much more than grades, as we just discussed—they are a chance to set benchmarks. My children may have stuffed their report cards in their sock drawers after the quarter was over, but I know for a fact they still look back at them with pride. And this is where the narrative element moves beyond letter grades to tell the story of who your student is becoming. Looking back at old report cards as the teacher, it is hard to believe when my son was in third grade that my biggest concern for him was X or my greatest hope was Y—when now that seems pale in memory and what I hope for his future is so much more brilliant. Using report cards to tell the story of our children's progress through the year (and years) blesses not only the student, it blesses the teacher. In a job where there are no promotions, a tangible means of measuring our students' growth over time through the narrative of their journey is the most satisfying reward there is.

GRADES

Moving on to grades, if you are new to teaching (and even if you aren't) it might be a bit of a mystery how to keep track of grades while homeschooling. Historically, grading has not been a fundamental part of homeschooling, since many parent teachers were able to assure mastery in their own student—that seemed like enough. As a result, there is a large variance among curriculum companies when it comes to assessment. Some online or computerized curriculums provide automatic grading, while more traditional curriculums make tests and quizzes available for additional purchase. Other curriculums offer no tests at all. Develop your own healthy philosophy of how you want your family to handle grades, and select curriculums that will work well with your choice.

SIMPLE IS BETTER

My best advice about grades is to keep it simple. There are typically three components to grades, and as you may recall from your education that every teacher weighs them differently—likewise, plan to set your own guidelines. Those three components are classwork, assignments (such as projects or papers), and tests. Broadly speaking, grades for younger students are weighted more toward classwork and class participation, and older students' grades are weighted more toward assignments and tests. But it is really up to the teacher.

SOONER > LATER

For parents considering when to start including grades, sooner is often better than later. By incorporating grades in the early elementary years, you accomplish two things: First, you begin to acclimate your student to the idea that there are academic expectations at home. Second, you give yourself a window of time to practice developing a grading system that works for you before you get into the more critical upper elementary grades, and certainly by high school. This gives you plenty of time to try different options, to ask questions of other home-schoolers in your community, and to land on a system that meets your family's needs before grading becomes more essential.

STATE STANDARDS

As we lead into talking about building your own grading system, I encourage you to look up your state's standards at the beginning of your school year so you know what the state expects of students at your child's grade level. It's a good starting point for keeping your own expectations realistic. (Do an online search for "_____ state education standards grade _____" and see what you find.) Once you learn how to wade through the education terminology of Objectives (which is another way of saying what teachers hope to accomplish that year), summaries, and reports (which are often different ways to restate the conclusion) you will be able to write alongside each standard where you satisfied those needs in the course of your regular classwork.

RUBRICS

Let's talk briefly about rubrics—a common education term meaning how something will be graded. It sounds a lot harder than it is. In the culinary world, we would call a rubric a recipe—it's what the student needs to do to earn the full grade.

Many schools traditionally use a percentage system where A's are 100–90, B's are 89–80 and so on. We eventually worked our way up to letter grades, but when my children were in early elementary, I used check marks because that was sufficient. I could easily give my students feedback on an assignment by putting a check at the top (to show it was completed), a check+ (on the rare occasion that they knocked it out of the park), a check- (if they skipped some of the work or clearly didn't try), or a minus (if they skipped or lost the assignment). At the end of the quarter, checks were worth 10 points, a check+ 11, a check- 9, and a minus was a 5. I would average the points and give them a percentage. As we added quizzes and tests into the mix, I would average those separately and then average classwork and tests together.

This became an instant motivator for the kids, almost like a game. They wanted to win. They would peek over my shoulder while I graded each page, celebrating if they got a check and double celebrating if it was a check+. They know our love for them is not tied to their performance, and just like we cheer for them to score high in soccer, we cheer for them to score high in spelling. By explaining our rubric to our children ahead of time, they understood what they needed to do practically to win the game—and it helps keep the assessment in perspective.

As your kids move into junior high and high school, consider keeping check marks for homework assignments, and awarding numerical grades for all other projects and tests. I have chosen a curriculum that provides tests and quizzes, shows me how much each problem is worth when I am grading it so they all add up to 100%, and gives me an answer key, because that is what I prioritize. You may think differently.

In English, for example, I have chosen a writing curriculum that gives my third grader a list of tasks to complete on each writing assignment, such as the sample rubric shown here, so she knows where to put her focus when she writes her paragraph.

Even though my curriculum does not assign grade values to its rubric, because it is clearly organized I can still use it to assign point values for each category. When considering high school curriculum, look for companies that offer even more detailed rubrics for assignments.

Sample Rubric: 3rd Grade Paragraph

Title .... ☐

All capitalization rules followed .... ☐

4–7 Complete sentences .... ☐

3 Interesting adjectives .... ☐

3 Interesting adverbs .... ☐

Correct spelling .... ☐

Correct punctuation .... ☐

RECORD KEEPING

Keeping track of grades requires only a sheet of paper. If this is your first quarter with grades, put a page in a binder for each of your children and list their subjects down the side. Beside each subject, write down their check or grade as each assignment is completed. Others prefer to go digital by entering grades into a spreadsheet, which can even be updated from a phone. With all the balls we are juggling, define grading simplicity for yourself. At the end of the quarter, if you have checks in one column and numbers in another, average them separately and then average them together. Or provide more weight for one category than the other—it's up to you. Remember, you are in charge.

If this is your first year homeschooling, leave breathing room for some early wins. If the best you can do with grades for your elementary student in the first quarter is to make your best guess if your student did A, B, or C level work in each subject based on classwork and daily goals, great! He will still love that you saw his work and paid attention to his growth and needs. He doesn't need to see your tally chart to know how you got there. Even if your student is in junior high or high school, give yourself a month or two to get the hang of things with "warm-up grades."

Finally, it's important to clarify that grades are a private thing in our family. I return graded tests and exams to each of my students individually, I protect my grade book from prying eyes, and we discuss report cards privately. My husband and I sit down with our children as individuals to encourage, correct, and listen to them as we hash out together what they need to do or receive to succeed in school. Part of the reason why shame has not tainted the grade cycle for our children is that we have provided a safe space for them to fail and achieve. Of course, when they earn straight As, they hang it on the fridge, call their grandparents, and tell the checkout lady at the grocery. And we are great with that.

> Tests provide me with valuable information about my child's gaps and progress.

TESTS

Around third grade, we begin to include tests in our curriculum: math, language, and spelling, especially. (Except for my youngest, who asked if she could please start having math and spelling tests early with her older siblings.) We also begin writing paragraphs and book reports with scoring around third grade.

If we view "test" as another word for trial or challenge, we come to see that we're surrounded by them every day. While I agree that bubbles and #2 pencils are rarely used outside of a classroom, the principles of preparing for a challenge, retooling ourselves to digest new information, learning how to cope and perform under pressure, and being capable of accepting both positive and negative feedback about our results are all practical life skills.

ROUTINE

Making tests part of your weekly routine may eventually deemphasize whatever stress you anticipate your child may feel from them. In addition to standard formats like fill-in-the-blank or multiple choice, a test might be asking your child to give an oral report or write an essay after reading a book. Variety is helpful, especially if your child has special learning needs so you can make accommodations.

Depending on where you live, your state may require your children to take national exams at some point. Some states allow parents to choose a brand of test from a short list, and for parents in charter programs (see Chapter 9) the tests are paid for by the school. By this point in the book I suspect you know your state's requirements on this topic, but if not, check out "Links to Experts" on HomeschoolExpert.com.

RECOMMENDED

While we have certainly complied with our state's requirements to turn in scores every few years, I have also opted to test my kids every year for my own assessment purposes. Following second grade, our children take two national exams annually that are commonly approved on state lists. This accomplishes three things. First, it gives my kids practice taking a national exam on a regular basis to help de-stress the process and give them confidence. Second, it provides a record of their progress and growth should we ever want to give proof of education. Third—and, in my mind, most important—the tests provide me with valuable information about my child's gaps and progress.

A glance at their overall scores shows me which subjects need a bit more attention in the coming school year, or maybe even over the summer. It also provides information to me about whether some training in test prep would be helpful. And as with everything else, my husband and I keep the results private between ourselves and each student, with the exception of the years when our district requires we mail in the scores.

END OF YEAR BINDER

Finally, the End of Year Binder This is the original tool I used for measuring progress before we included report cards, and is one I continue to use. In our Chapter 7 discussion of school supplies, I explained that I keep a folder for each student in my teacher box to save samples of their work. This is where those folders come in handy.

WORK SAMPLES

At the end of the year, I put together a binder for each student that is a visual summary of the year. I include a few assignments, some art they have created, their report cards, and state exams. If we go on field trips or build a crazy project, we turn those into short writing assignments and print them, with photos, to go in the binder.

My children practically glow with pride at all they have accomplished when I present them with their binders at the end of the year. I love watching them flip to the start and find math pages that brought them to tears earlier in the year which now look so easy to them, or the way they wrote their names in September that by June they think looks juvenile. Even in junior high, my students go back to their earlier binders, reminding themselves that what was hard then is easy now—inspiring them that what is hard now is probably going to get easier too.

> The success of our children as students and adults is not a validation of our success as their teachers.

They see their own progress without me having to tell them, and they almost seem to grow another inch just looking at it. And, selfishly, it ups my credentials in their estimation. The next time I hand out writing assignments that seem overwhelming and impossible, I point back to a project early in the previous year—especially one where tears were involved—and remind them how hard that seemed then yet how doable it is now. It has been a tangible means to earn their trust as the teacher.

STATE STANDARDS

In addition to showing a collection of their work—and this is, frankly, the part that takes the most time—I do a side-by-side comparison of our state's education standards for their grade level and where our children have met or exceeded them. In the first few years of homeschooling, with my husband being new to education at home, this piece was especially compelling for him and helped alleviate his concerns about whether or not our children were falling behind.

It was worth the time, not only to make certain I was providing a thorough education for our children, but to keep open communication on the topic between my husband and me. Especially if you choose to never give a grade or test, I encourage you to build a binder for each of your kids.

FINAL THOUGHTS

In our performance-driven world, it is encouraging to me to discover how our children find joy in challenging themselves to grow and in seeing proof of their own growth. Teaching our children to approach and prepare for a challenge, push themselves, give it their best, and make use of the results is an incredibly valuable life skill, no matter where our children aim in future schooling or careers.

Report cards are just the start. I never thought I'd be grateful for them, but in many ways it is a highlight of our quarter. As your child progresses and grows, I hope it will be for you too. When we step back to look at the big picture, it is important to remind ourselves that the success of our children as students and adults is not a validation of our success as their teachers; our children are not an end product, they are in process—as we all are.

We all face tests and grades daily, even if they aren't printed on a card with A's and B's. Training our children to face life's tests with teachability and confidence is a gift.

11

How Do I Know If My Child's Learning Needs Are Typical or Specialized?

Spotting and Supporting Special Learning Needs

From the time we welcome our babies into our homes, we become students of them. The question, "Is this normal?" becomes a regular part of the growing up years as we seek to provide and protect as best as parents can. Especially with the first child, it is difficult to know when walking at 10 months versus 14 months is a big deal, how many teeth they should have by 18 months, and what is the right vocabulary for a 2-year-old, just to name a few. We do our best to stay informed and keep calm. But sometimes ... sometimes there is a nagging feeling of, "This isn't right."

Before launching further into this discussion, let me be circumspect for a moment. This is a sensitive and important topic for many families. One of the times as parents when we feel least qualified for the job is when we discover that our child may have needs that require extra support in an area we know little to nothing about. As homeschoolers responsible for the role of parent and teacher, parents want to know if their child's academic struggles are typical or a sign of something more serious, what they should look for that would indicate a need for additional help, if or how to have their child diagnosed, where to find help if it's needed, and whether it's even possible to homeschool while supporting those needs at home. These are all really important questions.

This is where our team of experts is such a great resource. This chapter will share advice and best practices from professional educators, child psychologists, and specialized therapists. You are not alone in this, and we will talk about how to build a strong support team for you and your child. While this information comes from experts, I am not a medical professional and I encourage you to pursue professional help for your child if you believe it is warranted.

Homeschooling can be a meaningful way to create a nurturing, customized learning environment for children with special needs that helps them reach their full potential. I know this from firsthand experience.

TRUST YOUR GUT

It's best to start this conversation with the initial question, "Does my child need additional support, and is it possible for me to homeschool her if she does?"

The short answer is, with the help of experts, yes. Many parents of children with special needs ranging from Down's Syndrome to dyslexia, blindness to paralysis, or deafness to Asperger's have found success educating their children at home—especially with the right supports in place.

> Be willing to advocate for your child, sourcing as many opinions as are necessary until your concerns about your child's struggles are answered sufficiently.

Before we can talk about support systems, let's start with the question that comes before it, which is, "Does my child need additional support?" Not all special learning situations are initially obvious.

The first step in answering that question about whether or not your child needs additional support is to trust your gut. As a parent who has experienced that unsettling feeling that something with this child is a lot harder than it was with the others, my first recommendation is to seek professional help. Be willing to advocate for your child, sourcing as many opinions as are necessary until your concerns about your child's struggles are answered sufficiently. It could simply be that your child is developing in a healthy way on his own timeline—children read, grow, and learn at their own pace and in their own way. Slowness is not necessarily an indication of a problem, but it is worth monitoring in the event help of some kind is needed later.

It was my husband who first connected the dots about Sam. Sam is incredibly bright, talkative, and cuddly. But Sam struggled with sensitivities, tasks, and transitions in ways our other children did not. Around the age of 3, I discussed these dots with our pediatrician.

Unfortunately, the pediatrician did not see the same concerns with Sam's development and suggested we follow up in a year. In learning from experts in this field since then, they consistently encourage parents to begin with the pediatrician and continue on to a specialist if the parent's concerns are not adequately addressed. Many pediatricians respond to this line of questioning from parents with the best intentions but may not be specialists and therefore cannot be 100% accurate because they are not trained in diagnosing this complex issue.

Since our questions hadn't been answered completely, we tracked down a pediatric psychologist who diagnosed Sam over a series of interviews. That was the day our lives changed—and changed, I would argue, for the better. It is not that the doctor handed Sam a challenge that did not already exist; the doctor gave us handlebars in the form of a diagnosis so we could help steer and support Sam more effectively.

Less dramatic, but just as helpful, was the day our child Alex was diagnosed with dyslexia and significant visual impairment. We were able to put some learning solutions, coaching, and assistive technology into place that made learning more effective for Alex.

INDICATORS THAT HELP IS NEEDED

At this point in the conversation, many parents ask, "What are common indicators I should look for that my child needs additional support?"

It is a well-intended question, but given the diversity of psychological or physical learning needs a child might present, there is no way to adequately address that in one chapter. As Autism specialist Patricia Schetter pointed out to me, "When you have seen one child with Autism you have only seen one child with Autism." Even within the singular diagnosis of Autism Spectrum Disorder (ASD) there is a vast array of ways a child could present with that need.

Out of respect for the complexity of learning needs, as well as parents' need for help, I developed a resource section under "Links to Experts" at Homeschool-Expert.com that will help launch your search, as well as podcasts with experts on the topic. If you are ever concerned that your child may need additional support, there is no harm in asking your pediatrician. If the worst-case scenario is discovering your child's needs are typical, that is a great worst-case scenario—all it cost you was a doctor's appointment.

TO DIAGNOSE OR NOT?

All this leads to the sensitive question of whether or not to diagnose.

There are diverse perspectives on this topic. Over the years I have spoken with many parents of students who have unique learning needs. Almost always, parents who choose not to seek help do so because they are concerned about labeling and, therefore, inhibiting the growth of their child. Or they believe that by homeschooling their child without a diagnosis they will be able to provide enough customized support at home that a diagnosis is not necessary. I can certainly respect both perspectives. While I realize this is a personal and sensitive topic, allow me to say that for our family the label was a gift.

For us, a diagnosis was not a limitation; it gave us clarity, support, and wings—especially when it was handled discreetly with friends in the early years. Unfortunately, there is a significant amount of misinformation on some categories of special learning needs. If a child is born with one leg shorter than the other and needs surgery to help it grow straight, nearly every parent I know would do whatever was possible to get the surgery done. But for some reason, when it comes to psychological needs, enthusiasm for giving the child mental and emotional support is less consistently embraced.

Whether in homeschool or traditional school, diagnosing and supporting learning needs (as well as physical and psychological support) early on is incredibly beneficial to developing a holistically healthy child. Arguably, homeschooling makes a great platform for addressing the social implications of psychological and learning needs by removing academics from potentially challenging social environments. Research continues to show that early intervention is best in helping children overcome challenges in a positive, supportive environment.

For parents who don't intend to use any of the support structures available to students who share your child's symptoms, I agree that it probably doesn't make sense to pursue a diagnosis. For parents who desire outside help because they feel like they are doing their best and it still isn't working, getting professional support is worth getting the diagnosis.

ANOTHER WAY TO THINK ABOUT SUPPORT

Reframing our family's learning needs as a different story helped me consider it from a new perspective when we were trying to make this decision. All four of my children have genetically challenged teeth, with a misaligned bite that causes negative wear and tear. I am grateful we are able to access orthodontia for them so that, by getting help early while their jaws are still growing, they can develop in a healthy, supported way that will save my kids from painful jaw and migraine issues in the future, not to mention the potential need for surgery as adults.

Similarly, Sam was born with a way of thinking and responding to the world that is challenging at times, and different from what we typically experience in society. If I am willing to get Sam braces to support the healthy growth of jaw and teeth, why wouldn't I pursue the psychological and educational supports Sam needs to develop healthy growth in confidence, intelligence, and abilities?

Prior to Sam's diagnosis, I knew very little about Sam's specific type of learning needs. It was overwhelming at first—I wanted to get it right for Sam's sake but didn't know where to start. And that is why I recommend getting professional help early on—it was a game changer for us. Sam has grown so much in various areas as a result of the coaches and therapists we involved in Sam's education. I am confident that we would not have gotten to where we are today without them. And having experts involved in Sam's development reduced my inner turmoil as parent teacher, worrying if I was missing something Sam needed.

> For us, a diagnosis was not a limitation; it gave us clarity, support, and wings.

WHY A DIAGNOSIS HELPS

With a diagnosis in hand, homeschooling became a lot easier. Depending on your child's learning needs, you can access reading specialists, speech therapists, applied behavioral analysts, physical and occupational therapists, psychologists, and more. There is a large team of experts ready to assist you with the customized support you need to teach your child well, often funded through your school district or insurance company.

A diagnosis for your child will also support how the state perceives your student's national exam scores. This is especially important if you live in a state that requires homeschoolers to submit results, or if your student plans to apply to college and chooses to legitimize all he has learned beyond standard academics by supplying the university with that information. A diagnosis will also make a big difference if your student plans to take nationally recognized exams such as the SAT or AP tests, in the event she needs accommodations during the exam that would improve her chances of scoring well. No one expects you to do this alone—there is a team of experts just waiting for you to ask for help.

WHERE TO FIND HELP

Where can you find these experts? Fortunately, new support networks have developed alongside increased awareness of special learning needs.

In addition, if your family has medical insurance, call your insurance company to ask for a list of providers who can *test* for learning disabilities or physical needs. In my early searches, I found many in-network providers who would *provide therapy*, but locating someone to complete the costly evaluations required more sleuthing on my part. A pediatric psychologist, educational therapist, speech therapist, developmental pediatrician, ENT, or ophthalmologist may be a good place to start, depending on the need.

(Expert tip: If there are no diagnosticians within your medical plan in your area, some insurance companies allow you to request an exemption to see someone out of network with in-network coverage, so it's worth asking.)

> Subtracting friends from schoolwork helped Sam succeed at both by focusing on those areas separately rather than simultaneously.

Even as a homeschool parent, you may also be able to access help through your school district, which may be obligated to offer support to special needs students. If you decide to go this route, reach out to the guidance counselor at your local school for direction. From there, if your child requires a diagnosis, those teams may be able to direct you to the necessary resources.

Please take into account that, initially it may require some perseverance and a few closed doors before you find your open door (especially if you are seeking help for learning disabilities); keep at it.

EARLY IS BEST

One of the questions parents ask next is, "What is the right age for me to pursue an evaluation for my child—is it better if I wait until he is older and has better cognitive skills?"

Historically that answer was often yes, but times have changed. Psychologists now assert that early diagnosis is best, and the tools used for evaluation and diagnosis are incredibly sensitive in their approach. Experts in this field agree that, similar to my orthodontia analogy, the earlier they are able to accommodate and support a child's needs, the broader the positive effect will ultimately be for the child's well-being.

In other words, there is almost no age too young to begin asking questions. If you think your child has a vision issue at 18 months, get it checked. One of my children saw the pediatric ophthalmologist starting at three months of age for vision challenges based solely on family history and was monitored quarterly. It is better to ask the professionals as early as you spot the need or difference rather than to wait until it is significantly pronounced.

For us, subtracting friends from schoolwork during the day has helped Sam succeed in both areas by focusing on those needs separately rather than simultaneously.

Sam was diagnosed at age 3, and we chose to keep Sam's diagnosis a secret from friends and family. We are proud of Sam and love Sam for who Sam is; however, we also recognize that socially there is a fair amount of ignorance still around diagnostic labels that might make it harder for Sam to make friends if that information was public. Sam is high functioning, and we wanted to raise the bar and provide support for whatever Sam needs to reach full potential.

Though we haven't discussed it publicly, we have been devoted behind the scenes to getting Sam every kind of support and help needed with a variety of coaches that, at times, have been in our lives up to three or four times a week for months or years at a time.

We have been proactive in getting Sam the best help possible as early as we spot a need so that Sam sees those differences as an asset. We chose to cushion any social or academic concerns we had about the label by being discreet about the diagnosis. In fact, I don't even have a child named Sam or Alex, though this is a true story about two of our children's needs. Their stories are for them to tell, not me.

DIFFERENT IS NOT LESS

One benefit of studying your child's learning strengths early on is that it sets a healthy tone at home that we are all made differently. Just as a Kinesthetic learner is no better or worse than a Visual learner, so is a student with Autism no better or worse than a student without. We are all different, not less. Dr. Temple Grandin is a professor at Colorado State University and one of the first individuals on the Autism spectrum to document her experience. She is a remarkable woman who regularly speaks to the needs of people with Autism (she applied her expertise to the humane treatment of livestock), and has popularized that motto, "Different, not less."

All our children have the capacity for creativity and good, and it is our job to first discover and respect how they are made so that second, we can do everything possible to help push them forward in their strengths and grow through their weaknesses. For all of us, our greatest strength is often the flip side of our greatest weakness. And "normal" is often wrongly overvalued as "healthy."

Going back to my orchard illustration, if one of my saplings produces pine cones and another pineapples, it would be ridiculous of me to consider one less than the other. Of course, it would require a whole new kind of gardening know-how and greenhouse setup to adapt from nurturing one tree versus the other, but that speaks more to *my* learning opportunity as the gardener and *not* to the tree.

JUST ONE

Let me pause for a moment for a word of encouragement. That word is: One. As you consider the vast spectrum of special learning needs, reassure yourself that you only need to solve for one child. You don't need a degree in every kind of learning need that exists, you just need to study your one child, get some professional tools for your one child, and experiment with those tools to decide which fit your one child best.

ONE FOR ALL

Adapting our homeschool environment to meet the needs of our diagnosed child had some unexpected benefits. Where Sam's needs required structure, routine, and clarity, I discovered that meeting those needs had a positive impact on our other children. For example, because Sam struggled with processing the concept of time, I began to regularly use visual timers, Time Ladders, and a visual daily schedule to manage our day. (See Chapter 7 for details on those tools. Our visual daily schedule is available for free in Lesson 1 of *Homeschool Like an Expert: Video Series*.) Many of the tools I developed to help Sam, I did in collaboration with our various experts to make sure I was producing what Sam needed. After Alex was diagnosed, we incorporated those adaptations into our routine as well.

The surprise for me came a few months into our new routines when I discovered my other children were significantly benefiting from the new systems in their independent time management, working efficiency, and increased comprehension. To test the application of these tools further over the years, I presented them to homeschool groups in the Silicon Valley and Seattle with positive results. It turns out that what Sam and Alex needed was just a magnified version of what other students needed too.

Beyond charts and laminated instructions, our family has developed a new vocabulary around how we use our words to express needs, request personal space, explain hurt, and practice forgiveness and patience with each other. As challenging as it has been at times to stretch ourselves to accommodate each other's differences, it has given us the opportunity to learn resilience together.

Being under the same roof as we learn to work through these learning challenges has been sandpaper on some days and celebration on others. Even on the days when we couldn't finish our math work because of some unplanned, self-made crisis, the kids grew more from learning how to love each other in the face of adversity than by learning how to reduce fractions that day. Our family operates as a team, and when we help one team member get stronger, the whole team gets stronger. As the French author Alexandre Dumas famously wrote, "All for one and one for all."

Yes, we continue to study fractions. But we also keep the big picture in mind—that strength begets strength. That as we submit ourselves to the challenge of learning and working with each other's strengths (and, likewise, have patience with ourselves and each other in our weaknesses) we are building future adults who will be equipped to balance responsibilities, value relationships, and handle real-world needs.

One of the big lessons I have learned from Sam and Alex is that all of us have special needs in some way, and our own different preferences for how we learn best. As Temple Grandin points out, different is not less.

> The kids grew more from learning how to love each other in the face of adversity than by learning how to reduce fractions that day.

FINAL THOUGHTS

My hope is that you will turn the page on this chapter feeling empowered and encouraged. Because you know and love your child better than anyone, your ability to adapt these resources to meet your child's needs is stronger than you may give yourself credit. Remember: You don't have to understand and accommodate every kind of special learning need in the world, you just need to help this one. And because homeschooling is flexible and adaptable by nature, you may discover that accommodating your student at home is straightforward.

Many parents who have chosen to homeschool their child with special learning needs have praised education at home for enabling them to raise the bar of possibilities for their child while providing needed support. They have also celebrated how it removes social shame from the equation so their child can practice to learn, fail, and succeed at home.

You are in charge of your child's needs, and with help from experts you are going to do great.

12

How Do I Balance Multiple Ages at the Same Table?

Toddlers Through Teens, and Everything in Between

M any families teach more than one child at home, and when there is a wide age range it can require some creative juggling on the part of the parent teacher.

Parents ask, "How am I supposed to teach my teenager chemistry while keeping my toddler from going on a self-guided tour of our cleaning supplies? How do I create a studious environment for more challenging subjects when my youngest is belting out show tunes from the family room? How do I make homeschooling work when I feel like I am neglecting both by not being enough for either?"

These are heartfelt questions that go beyond keeping our children entertained to providing for them individually, intentionally, and creatively no matter their age. For this lesson, I've combined advice from dozens of homeschoolers with large families with my own experience teaching four children spanning eight years of age, with eight tips about juggling time, developing tools, and making learning inviting so that homeschooling a wide age range is doable.

1) LEARNING IS A LIFESTYLE

While some days are certainly easier than others when teaching a range of ages in the home, there are benefits to developing a holistic learning lifestyle that go beyond academics to developing students who are relational. We tell our kids that they are "friends for life," and although we encourage friendships beyond the home, we have made it clear that these four friends under our roof are worth the investment of time because they will be together all the rest of their days.

Sometimes I must remind myself of this principle too, when I am modeling for my children my relationships with my adult siblings or mediating yet another property dispute with my children. Teaching them to communicate, not only by speaking to each other but by listening and empathizing, is a life skill that will serve them well in adulthood.

2) JUGGLE TIME

This is where the flexibility of your Time Ladder, which we discussed back in Chapter 7, will serve you best. It will help you almost be multiple places at once keeping your children on task with clear expectations even if you can't be in the same room. Some families have chosen to adapt their Time Ladders by creating space for their older children's schooling on the right of the time column and their younger children's activities on the left, helping to pace the day between the two age groups.

There are benefits to developing a holistic learning lifestyle that go beyond academics to developing students who are relational.

If you have older students in junior high and high school, the good news is that many of their subjects will require smaller concentrated chunks of time with you, such as 5 to 15 minutes for clarification or direction to go over the material before the student heads off to complete the remainder of the work independently.

Many experienced homeschool parents recommend a streamlined system of learning for older students with four steps: First, the student discusses the assignment before beginning. Second, he completes the assignment independently, asking questions as needed. Third, the student shows the completed assignment to his parent. If it is a composition, such as an essay, his parent can correct it later. However, if it is a subject with an answer key, the student can move to the fourth step--grading the work himself while under parent observation. Not only does this develop a sense of autonomy in the student while maintaining accountability, it also helps him get quicker feedback on the assignment.

If you have older students in upper elementary grades, the good news is that your school day requires less work overall and subjects can often be broken into smaller chunks to make the day more manageable. Many families of multiples will get the younger students engaged in an activity and use that time to work 1:1 with their eighth grader on math for 15 minutes or until the younger child needs attention. At that point, the teacher parent will turn to the eighth grader and assign that child a chore break or two while the parent works with the younger child.

Some families find that it's easier for the Bigs to focus on tough subjects during the Littles' nap time. By balancing between the two different schedules of Littles and Bigs throughout your day, you can create pockets to meaningfully engage with both.

When I had four under the age of 8, and the youngest two were napping, I would take turns between the 8-year-old and 6-year-old working for 15 minutes with one while the other played quietly or did a chore so that we could have some special time to work alone and more efficiently. Every 15 minutes I would flip-flop between the boys until the girls woke up from their naps.

Not only did we get our work done faster, this made learning feel really special to the boys during a season in our family's life when they weren't always the first child to get my attention, and it was one of the ways I was intentional about meeting their "love tank" needs during our day. I even named it "Special Learning Time with Mom" to make it feel special. And, it did. As the boys are now growing up and moving into their own lives, I treasure that time I set aside to be with them independently during their younger years.

3) BUSY BOXES

Here she goes again, with another flashy name for something. Yes, I admit that I lean on the glitter of fun names for things readily in our house. (It must come with being a poet.) And I bet you might even be willing to admit that you want to see what's inside the Surprise Busy Box too, don't you? With a name like that, so will your younger students.

Giving activities an exciting name gives them Wow Power, like our Special Time incentive I talked about earlier. The purpose of the Surprise Busy Box is that this is something special for the younger siblings that only comes out when the older siblings are doing school. The contents should be desirable, creative, and safe for the child to explore alone.

I used to rotate the contents of the Surprise Busy Box regularly to keep it engaging for my Littles. A few ideas of what my children enjoyed in the box were dough, markers, toy cars, bubbles, pipe cleaners, big beads with lacing, or some favorite books with audio guides. Of course, everything was nontoxic, safe, or washable.

In addition to the Busy Box, which my Littles could play with solo, I developed a Busy School Box to keep at the school table with special cutting printouts I got online for free, safety scissors, plastic cups for sorting, and fuzzy craft balls for dividing between the cups. One of my daughter's favorite school table activities was sitting in her high chair alongside the big kids with some contact paper and tissue paper confetti—she loved sticking them together. Basically, I used whatever I could find to build stations throughout my house that enabled my toddler to explore textures safely, quietly, and without too much mess.

One of my kids' favorite boxes was the Bean Box. I bought a wholesale bag of dried pinto beans (or sometimes rice), buried some toy cars and figurines in the bottom, and let them search, recover, and re-bury. Even though we had a few beans underfoot at the end, it was a team favorite. Preschools, occupational therapists, and rehabilitation specialists have all commented on the value of this sort of exercise for young children as well as children with sensory processing needs; it is soothing, calming, and safe (especially when using rice).

Expert tip: I recommend putting the Bean Box on a sheet for easy clean-up and salvaging later. Expert tip, cont: That works great for Legos too! For parents concerned about sandboxes (such as their silicates or vacuum cleaner destruction capabilities), the indoor Rice Bin has also been an edible, cleanable, environmentally friendly win.

Whatever playbox you create that interests your younger child, I encourage you to diligently reserve it for school time only, so it maintains its power to captivate. It is always easier to direct Littles toward a quiet, positive activity than it is to pull Littles away from a loud, distracting activity.

4) MEDIA

One of the third ways I could engage our Littles meaningfully from time to time while doing school with the Bigs was through media. Used sparingly and appropriately, there are shows available through streaming media, the library, or PBS that have been engaging younger audiences with meaningful content for years, such as puppet, musical, or immersion language learning programs. There are also excellent apps available for tablets and phones that reinforce preschool concepts about shapes, colors, patterns, and sorting.

Please understand, I am not suggesting you set your toddler in front of a screen all day or even a little bit every day. There is plenty of research being done about the negative impact of screen time and social media on the healthy neurodevelopment of children, so I encourage you to spend any minutes on tech carefully. That said, if a moment arises when you need to park your Little somewhere to be safely occupied, this can be a good alternative.

5) PREP AHEAD!

As with nearly everything in life, the results of our efforts are significantly better with advance planning and prepping. When you have learning materials ready to go, you can be on the alert for moments in the day when your youngest becomes enraptured watching the garbage truck out the window, giving you 5 to 10 minutes to sit down with your oldest and go over work together.

I cannot encourage you enough to organize your student assignment calendars and resources at the beginning of the week, and to know what materials are required for your day before you sit down to Morning Meeting. It will give you the feeling of driving and thriving in your own day instead of surviving someone else's.

Along with planning ahead academically, the stress of getting out the door on time went down significantly when we incorporated "Ready, Break!" into our Morning Meeting. For a refresher on that, please see Chapter 7.

> Giving activities an exciting name gives them Wow Power.

6) INVITE LITTLES

A sixth principle in structuring your days between the age groups is to create ways to invite the Littles into your learning space whenever possible. The spiral method of education exposes younger children to educational content multiple times in their academic career even before they are able to fully grasp it, preparing their minds to engage that content more successfully as they get older. It plays on the timeless principle of the youngest child in the family growing up the fastest, learning from and trying to keep up with all the older siblings.

Again, experienced homeschool parents weigh in strongly on this one. Invite the Littles to snuggle with you while you read history and literature to the Bigs, or encourage your youngest to color in a high chair while older siblings work at the school table so he can feel big, too, and maybe absorb some content.

Some families develop Busy Boxes of beginner school supplies meant to be used only during school time at the school table so that the youngest can feel a part of things, scribbling and coloring in an older sibling's used workbook. (My preschoolers especially loved to color in their older siblings' used math workbooks. Many publishers incorporate a lot of color and shapes on to their pages to help students visualize math, and the preschoolers loved going through the images and circling their favorites to show me. They especially loved that their book was "real" and looked like the school books the older kids had. Bonus for me that it was free.)

7) WEEKEND DATES

In thinking more creatively about time, many families have made the age gap work by creating Weekend Dates. If there was a week when the distractions of the Littles made it impossible for me to finish a science experiment or history project with the Bigs, my husband would take our Littles to the park for a Weekend Date, giving me an hour or two to finish with the boys what we struggled to get done during the week.

This was actually a win for all the kids, because the girls felt like they had special time with my husband at the park and the boys enjoyed working with me distraction-free. We also tried to be intentional to flip it the next weekend, so that I could take the girls out for a Weekend Date to the park and my husband could do something fun with the older boys.

> Look for ways to enjoy this season, when the days are long and the years are short.

8) PLAY TEACHER

A common struggle many families face when the Bigs are mid-elementary and the Littles are toddler age is the desire of the older sibling to play teacher. So often, the teacher parent will be working with the preschooler on the sounds of letters when the older sibling jumps in to correct the younger, making it difficult for the younger to learn and creating all sorts of frustrating feelings for everyone.

There is a way to make this challenging scenario work to your advantage: First, celebrate the innate desire in your older child to lead or teach—it's an excellent life skill. Second, use this opportunity to coach him in his ability to lead with kindness and encouragement. Set aside time daily for him to read a picture book to your younger child, or to playfully reinforce a concept you taught your younger child earlier in the week.

There is a three-part learning cycle that includes exposure, mastery, and instruction. When we first gain knowledge, we are only being exposed to it (like the spiral method I mentioned above). Through time and practice, we master it. From there, once we have mastered the concept, we can turn around and instruct others. By inviting your older child into the learning space of the younger, you are giving both children an opportunity to enter that learning cycle together.

As you invite Bigs into the learning cycle, be sure to coach your older child about using encouragement rather than correction. Emphasize that it is more important to be a friendly teacher who celebrates and cheers than a discouraging teacher who just wants to show off how much they know.

Not only does Play Teacher provide a great character lesson, it also satisfies

190

the urge of the older sibling to get involved in the younger sibling's education. This will help you protect the rest of the time you need to work with your younger child individually. Consider giving the siblings' learning time together a special name, such as "Brother-Sister Time" so you can incorporate it into your visual schedule. When the older sibling wants to interrupt and help teach, you can encourage him to save it for "Brother-Sister Time" so that he is redirected instead of dismissed.

THE BIG PICTURE

Learning is a lifestyle. One of the easiest ways to make learning work with a wide range of ages is to keep your lifestyle simple. Try to minimize the number of outings in your week (and look for ways to share carpooling with other parents) and you will find that you not only get much more done but that your time together at home will also be more meaningful. Especially in the years with after-noon nap times, save as many errands as you can for the evening. (Plus, fewer outings often means a less stressed parent—for me, anyway—which was a greater benefit to my kids than one more outing.)

Admittedly, it used to drive me bananas when well-meaning grandparent types would approach me while out and about with my brood, encouraging me to soak up this season. At the time, the season felt exhausting—needing to be everyone's everything, sibling friction about the most inane disputes, dirty every-thing needing to be cleaned, and never enough sleep. The idea of trying to enjoy that season, in my more tired moments, seemed laughable.

Still, I took their message to heart, planning pockets of Special Time with each of my children during the week, and am so glad that I did. Those grandpar-ent types were right—time went by fast. Look for ways to enjoy this season, when the days are long and the years are short.

Education extends beyond academic assignments. When we look holistically at what our family is learning as we do life together, that larger view shows my children are learning adaptability, leadership through service, self-management skills, and consideration of others. Those life skills will serve them well wherever their future takes them.

The collaboration of my older children working with my youngers has gone far beyond the academic benefits of review and shared learning, though I have certainly seen educational gains from this model. My children are developing a friendship and sense of teamwork that will carry them together well into their adult years. Learning to love, live, and learn alongside each other has days of cele-bration and sandpaper—and all of them give us an opportunity to grow together.

13

Should I Homeschool Year-Round?

Making the Most of Vacations

O ne of the most common questions I get about homeschooling when I'm out in the community is whether I teach year-round. I think it's great that even non-homeschoolers see the potential of a flexible education. Some homeschool families do teach all year—especially those where both parents work outside the home full-time, and their solution is to do three-fourths of the work during the traditional school year and the remainder in the summer. The principles and tools in this chapter can be adapted to the vacations and holidays of the 12-month learning model. Just because our family schools during the traditional calendar months and has a Summer Learning Program during summer months does not mean your family has to do the same. Still, whenever you do find periods of rest, I encourage you to look for creative ways to make the most of them.

Play opportunities that bring learning to life in the off-season are among the highlights of our time together, not to mention a much-needed buffer for me as the teacher.

So, the short answer is: No, we don't homeschool year round. But we never stop learning.

DON'T YOU JUST NEED A BREAK?

Yes. And I take one. (In fact, I spend all of Lesson 9 talking about "Supporting the Teacher at Home" in the video series.) Before I get into the hows of summer learning, let's start with the whys.

As with many good things, it starts with a story. Way back when my oldest was in second grade, we studied division. And it was painful. All year he had loved math, but then we got to long division in spring and it nearly turned him against math for life. He understood and loved multiplication, but there was something backward and upside-down about all the steps of division that had him flustered. After two and a half months of teeth grinding and straining through long division, he got to the place where he could look at a page of division problems, shrug, and finish. It was glorious.

Then summer came, which was also glorious, and we welcomed fall naively with great hope now that we had conquered the dreaded long division. You see where this story is headed ... I will always remember that boulder-in-the-lap sense of defeat when the two of us sat down to start math in the fall and realized we had to learn long division *all over again*. With that rock in my lap, I promised myself I would never repeat that moment as a teacher.

> If this chapter feels like too much, scale it back to whatever makes sense for you and your family.

Does it require extra work on my part to create a teacher-free, modified Summer Learning Program? Yes. Would I rather just knock off school at the end of May and put my teacher hat in the closet until September? Yes. And would I hate myself that fall (especially now with review multiplied times the needs of four kids) for having to reteach all the basics they forgot in three months? You'd better believe it.

My Grandma used to say, "A stitch in time saves nine," and that old adage holds well for homeschool. I'd rather put forth minimal effort in the summer to maintain claim on what we earned and learned the hard way all school year than lose ground and have to recover it later.

Let's take a pause here: If life this past year was beyond stressful for you and this chapter feels like too much, scale it back to whatever makes sense for you and your family. Or if you feel like your child developed some significant learning gaps due to the rocky road of recent life, take this chapter a step further and use summer to double down and catch up. As with all my advice, please customize what I do for my family to fit what your family needs.

THAT SOUNDS EXHAUSTING

It might, but it really isn't. Especially if I get my summer material prepped by the end of May and if we make space for true breaks throughout the rest of the year.

Different from the year-round schooling model (where homeschoolers take two weeks off between quarters plus holidays, and then school with the regular curriculum the rest of the time), we modify our load in the summer. My goal in the summer is not to teach new concepts (again, I am building a teacher-free model on purpose); my goal is to make a space for my children to review, read, and explore on their own. Let's be honest: When I develop my kids' Summer Learning Program each year I am not just thinking of my kids—I am thinking of myself too. And that is a good thing! I need a break from being full-time teacher parent to restore myself and recharge for the fall, so I design a program that is both meaningful and kid-driven.

PART ONE: LEARNING PACKETS

Before summer starts, I build learning packets for each student. Oftentimes, I use whatever remnant worksheets we didn't need that school year as a starting place. If we have 10 weeks in summer, I make 10 packets (minus whatever weeks we might be traveling). The packets include a single math review page, a couple of sentences to diagram or edit for errors, a word search or word ladder (to support spelling), and some kind of science or geography detective worksheet.

If the results of my students' state exams that spring indicated a dip in a subject area, I'll add some extra work. If one child scored lower in geography, for example, I might print some maps for him to color and identify. I aim to have each packet take about an hour to an hour and a half to complete, and I give my kids one packet a week with seven days to complete it. Easy peasy. I check for completion only (no serious grading allowed). Because my students are reviewing material they've already studied, mistakes are minimal. And yes, I require that they finish their summer packets each week to maintain summer privileges. Packets are not optional.

PART TWO: SUMMER LEARNING PROGRAM

Second, I build a Summer Learning Program, which *is* optional and includes prizes. Honestly, my kids look forward to this one all year. (In fact, if my kids finish their school books early that year, they beg to have their summer list early so they can get started on it.) Here's why.

Years ago I listened to a great *Freakonomics* podcast with Steven Dubner on the value of incentives. Dubner observed that he could either pay hundreds of dollars to a summer program for his son to practice a language over break or he could pay his son far less to practice the language through an online program at home. And because his son was earning money to learn, he discovered his son was more motivated to finish the material than if he had attended the more expensive program with the tutor. It got me thinking: What would it be worth to push my kids into a new subject area over the summer?

Where might my kids be challenged to grow (like geography); where do they have natural interests or giftings we could advance (like computer programming)? Are there life skills they want to learn (like baking a pie) or extra chores they could tackle (like scrubbing grout throughout the house)? Granted, some of these my kids would do for free (like baking pies and coding) and others might require a little incentivizing (such as that geography workbook and grout). Even then, how much would it be worth to me to create a meaningful summer experience that is largely kid-driven?

For those who are opposed to paying their kids (I realize this is a sensitive topic; please see Chapter 7 for a discussion about chores and rewards) there is the option to earn extra privileges—tech time, a special date with Mom or Dad, or points toward a fun family outing. It could also be that the work itself is the prize—such as reading lots of books about backyard birds and squirrels, drawing his own art portfolio of what he observes, building a feeder together when he is done with all his "research," and having him draw and track in his portfolio which furry and feathered friends show up. Dream big. Summer is a great time to recover, relax, and grow in new ways—but it doesn't have to be hard on parent teachers.

READING

Reading is at the core of our Summer Learning Program. This is something my parents started with us as kids. Assigning us a total number of pages to read over the summer, my parents had us keep track of all the books we read each summer; if we met our page goal, we earned a $10 to $15 prize.

I adopted my parents' great summer reading idea and took it a step further. Once a year I curate a list of outside reading for each of our children by browsing state reading lists for their age level, looking at lists of award winners (such as Caldecott and Newberry), and checking out curriculum reading lists. If I am unfamiliar with titles on the list, I read a couple of quick reviews to make sure my child is emotionally ready for the content.

My goal in curating a list for them is to provide a spread of books across different genres, styles, and subject areas that are either at or slightly above their reading level. I want to stretch them. I want them to discover new interests by exposing them to titles they may not have otherwise considered. I picture myself as their tour guide through great reading and want to select landmarks along the way that I know will especially interest each child.

By reading the reviews of each book, I also feel more comfortable creating a list of books I haven't read. (Let's be real for a moment: There is *no way* I can read every book ahead of my four readers when there are great new books being published all the time). Online reviews have been incredibly helpful in temporarily steering me away from titles whose subject matter seemed too mature. Even some award-winning classics are quite mature on topics such as depression, violence, and suicide even though they are targeted at young readers. It's up to you as the parent to determine when you think your child is ready for those big topics and how to introduce them.

I arrange the books in different categories, trying to give choice points when possible. The first category is a short list of required reading to complete the program. From there is a list of biographies, and the program assigns a certain number to pick. Then there will be a list of historical fiction—choose X from here. Finally, there is a list of fabulous fiction with dozens and dozens of titles—pick X.

> Summer is a great time to recover, relax, and grow in new ways—but it doesn't have to be hard on parent teachers.

The beauty of this list is manifold, but I will just list two of the reasons. First, if there is a book we didn't get to in the spring for our curriculum, I put it in the required reading section to be sure it gets done. Second, this curated list becomes a resource I can use throughout the next school year or even roll into the next summer (or adapt in the future for a younger sibling); it's a year-round resource.

By arranging the books into categories, I encourage independence, autonomy, and choice; by providing categories in the first place, I am creating a helpful structure that exposes my reader to great books and makes the most of her summer learning. (Whatever titles she picks in the end are a win as far as I am concerned, because ultimately I selected all of them!)

Of course, if my students find books at the library they want to swap out for something on their list, I welcome that conversation (and have used it to teach them how to develop an eye for good books). The library is a big place. It's helpful to teach our children how to find great books so they can learn to do it for themselves. Over time, our kids develop a taste for great literature (we call them "steak" books at our house) and fun, fluffy books (we call those "brain candy"), and with practice they learn how to balance their own reading diet.

Summer Reading Programs can start at a very young age. When I had nonreaders, I built a chart of empty squares, where each square counted as a new book from the library that an adult read aloud. As our household grew to include young readers and nonreaders, I developed a space in the Bigs' Summer Reading Program to read a certain number of picture books aloud to the Littles. My Bigs developed oratory skills, my Littles had more family members reading to them, kids bonded—it was a win-win.

> Many families save summer for rocket launches, soda explosions, and hands-on science Mythbuster-style.

Consider setting up your program to include specific lists, page count goals, or book count goals—whatever is best for your family. At the end of the summer, I require my kids to have completed their summer packets. The summer reading list, though, is optional (and is often what they want to finish first) because they earn a prize at the end of the summer by completing it before school starts. Whatever your format, use summer to encourage all your students to explore reading.

ADDITIONAL LEARNING OPPORTUNITIES

This is where my *Freakonomics* story comes back in. During the first few summers when we had early readers, our Summer Learning Program was just a Summer Reading Program. But Dubner got me thinking: What could I offer my child as an incentive to dive deep into a subject over the summer and complete on her own, with no reminders from me?

I brainstormed ideas with the kids and we came up with a list of ways they could choose to earn money over the summer by pushing *themselves*. (This also, by the way, saved me from the annual lemonade and garage sale requests my little entrepreneurs were keen to host.) If they had a brand-new book of piano music ahead of them, I might offer a few dollars for them to memorize the book by fall—which, by the way, would require way more hours than their standard practicing times. Or we would set up benchmarks for learning to code, completing a certain number of levels on their typing program, or completing units in their online foreign language program. None of the Additional Learning Opportunities were for core subjects—they were all extras that rounded out their education, that didn't require an active role from me, and that might have been too much for us to address during the school year.

By the end of the summer, if I built the list creatively and designed the right incentives, I would achieve the following: kids who were busy and self-entertained with meaningful activities, a chance for my children to develop their work ethic and learn the value of a hard-earned dollar, on opportunity for my children to develop or strengthen skill sets and knowledge areas, a bit more peace and quiet around the house while they were occupied, children who were thrilled at the chance to earn money or prizes, and a break for me! Now you know why all of us look forward to the Summer Learning Program all year.

MESSY SCIENCE

There are some things I just don't want my kids to learn about in our kitchen—animal dissections is one of them. There is something about the smell of formaldehyde indoors without proper ventilation that has a way of seeping into the paint. However, that doesn't keep us from Messy Science—it means we just save it for summer! The great outdoors is the ideal place to host animal dissections, where there is plenty of fresh air and a hose if needed. Many families save summer for rocket launches, soda explosions, and hands-on science Mythbuster-style. If you didn't get to as much science during the school year as you would have liked, summer is a great time to build a model of the solar system to scale in the backyard with papier-mâché.

DO LESS

Along with giving you lots of ways to learn actively over the summer, I want to pair that with the encouragement to do less. Full-time parent teachers have a lot on their plates—especially if they are also homeschooling while employed. So look for ways to do less. Whether it is making easy meals on the barbecue, hosting a staycation instead of a vacation, reducing the number of activities your children join, or discovering new ways to relax together as a family (like late-night star gazing), do it. Make space to breathe and restore yourself. No one is going to ask you to turn in an essay in September about the amazing things you did with your summer; if rest and restoration are what would bless you most, do that. And save the bathroom remodel for another season.

Along this line of thinking: Don't be afraid of boredom in your children. Boredom is often the launching pad to creativity. Provide some creative outlets, like the Summer Learning Program and free play with friends, and then leave them with big pockets of unscheduled time to dream, think, make messes, and figure out how to clean it all up.

CREATIVE VACATIONS

There are many families who have used the flexibility of homeschooling to make the most out of family vacations. Some have gone to exotic international locations during off-peak seasons, others have enjoyed camping in national parks when the spots are less crowded during the traditional school year. There are all kinds of creative ways for homeschoolers to discover the world together as a family.

For example, I know of one family in the Pacific Northwest who took off a year from work, sold their house, loaded four young kids and survival gear onto bicycles, and biked around the U.S. (Yes, this was in the last 10 years). They had incredible adventures, schooled some core subjects along the way, and had an unforgettable year touring the country and deciding where to live when the year was done.

Another family of four had a tradition of Mom taking each fourth grader to Washington D.C. in the spring, just the two of them (after completing two years of American history and literature, writing a report to hand-deliver to her senator about a need in her state, and studying the nation's capital). It was a chance not only to celebrate what they had learned together so far, but to build special memories before transitioning into the teen years.

One of the families that inspired me as a young mom was a family with five children. During each of their children's junior high years, the parents guided their students into selecting a country to explore for the year. The student would learn as much about the country as possible—history, literature, economics, language, geography, etc.—and at the end of the year would spend three weeks in that country with one of the parents doing hands-on volunteer work and getting to know the people.

HAPPY REST

This chapter highlights tips for parents on how to take much-needed breaks to recharge, add buffers where needed, find and fill gaps during breaks to make the school year run smoother, and ease the back-to-school transition in the fall. However you choose to spend your seasons of rest, I hope they are just that— restful, a chance to catch your breath, and an opportunity to remember why you love life.

14

What is the University's
Perspective of Homeschoolers?

Expert Help from University Directors of Admissions

Y ears ago, "Dean Sue" Wasiolek from Duke University and I began discussing
an article that would speak to the university perspective of homeschoolers.
We were coauthoring the book *Getting the Best Out of College* with Peter
Feaver, a professor at Duke. Very little had been published at that point on the
topic of the college view of homeschoolers, so this past year we began to reach out
to admissions directors at universities nationwide to answer this question.

We were especially interested in speaking to deans and directors of admissions who had been working in that field over a few decades, in the hopes they
could share perspectives on what the initial view of homeschooled applicants
was when it first became legal and how (or if) that perspective has changed since.

We interviewed Christophe Guttentag (Dean of Admissions, Duke Universi-
ty), Steve Farmer (Vice Provost for Enrollment and Undergraduate Admissions,
University of North Carolina), Ronné Turner (Vice Provost for Admissions,
Washington University), and Noah Buckley (Director of Admissions, Oregon
State University). In addition to the experience all four experts have at their
current universities, their career histories in admissions extend to the University
of Pennsylvania, University of Virginia, Johns Hopkins University, Northeastern
University, University of Wyoming, and University of Maryland.

**WHAT WAS THE UNIVERSITY'S PERSPECTIVE OF HOMESCHOOLERS
ORIGINALLY?**

We gave all of our experts questions in advance so they could collect data ahead of our interviews, and each came in with clear recollections of perceptions then versus now.

All four deans agreed that back in the 1980s when homeschooling emerged there was a negative perception of homeschoolers—and, not just homeschoolers, but that diversity in general wasn't typically celebrated on college campuses. At that time, admissions officers read applications solving for the question, "Will this student fit into our culture?" The result, of course, was that colleges were much more homogeneous than they are today.

Dean Guttentag opened our conversation with his recollection: "I was just getting started in admissions and was sitting at the table with the Dean of Admissions for an Ivy League university. I recall the dean saying in regards to homeschooled applicants, 'We are unsure about the social adjustment of homeschoolers,' making it clear that admissions officers had a higher bar and that homeschoolers didn't fit within that norm. This was a time before charter schools, when education choices were limited. When parents chose to homeschool their children, the temptation on the part of the admissions officers was to be skeptical."

"...When parents chose to homeschool their children, the temptation on the part of the admissions officers was to be skeptical."

Since then, most universities have taken a different approach, looking to create a broader community within the student body that reflects the diverse world in which we live. It's not coincidental that college admissions began to transition to this broader mindset around the same time that the percentage of homeschoolers admitted increased.

"I am realizing now, just as we are talking about it," Dean Guttentag continued, "that the timeline on these histories is linked—colleges first tolerated then celebrated diversity. I think at the same time we began to value applicants coming from an environment that was different from the norm, that opened it up at the same time to homeschoolers as well. I think all those things happened at the same time, for the better."

On the other side of Tobacco Road, Vice Provost Farmer agreed, recognizing homeschool parents as being part of the solution: "People who worked in admissions 25 years ago were quicker to stereotype homeschool students because we thought we knew everything there was to know about them, and we really didn't. I think we have a much greater appreciation of applicants coming to us through alternative forms of education, and I think we have for a very long time now. I really believe homeschooled parents gave us the gift of slowing down.

They encouraged us to dig in and try to understand the student as a potential candidate instead of disregarding the application because it was outside the norm. We believe it is worth finding what is good and true and unique about each applicant. I would also add that, for sure, the number of homeschooled students we know about on campus is far less than the actual number. We only know who has been homeschooled coming out of high school if it is clear on their transcript or if they write about it in an essay. I suspect there are far more homeschoolers on campus than we realize."

All of our experts reflected the desire to be mindful of how campus life was changing for the better as universities look for ways to evaluate applications more holistically beyond test scores or traditional schooling methods. Vice Provost Turner at Washington University agreed, saying: "Over time, college admissions professionals have become more welcoming of homeschool applications. Way back when I first started, we were perplexed about how to measure applications of homeschooled students fairly. But as more institutions encountered more home-schooled applications, and as there became more advocacy, institutions worked hard to figure out how to best evaluate and support homeschool students."

Director Buckley at Oregon State University echoed Vice Provost Turner's sentiments, saying: "I think we've loosened up how we look at homeschooled applicants, going from what was once a skeptical view decades ago to now more of an interested curiosity. We are asking the question, 'What did this applicant do to really make education unique?' Many of these students are coming with really fascinating backgrounds and interesting stories, and there's a lot they can contribute to our campus. I can think of one family's story, of a dad who built huge pyrotechnic displays all around the country. He homeschooled his two boys while training them in this amazing business from a young age. His full-time job was really educating his sons, but they had the benefit of touring the country with him and setting up displays and learning so much from experience. Both boys went on to do great at the university as former homeschoolers."

It was clear in listening to each director talk about their teams that consider-ing applicants independently and holistically has required a significant increase in time spent evaluating students individually. Applications officers continue to look for ways to assess students fairly and accurately according to each student's learning background.

WHAT IS THE PERSPECTIVE NOW?

Universities are now eager to consider candidates not despite their uniqueness but because of it. Meaning, universities don't want students to seek out a learning opportunity solely because they think it will make them stand out from all the other applicants. All the experts agreed on this point. They emphasized that there are clear markers of authenticity and passion that come through in applications of students who pursued interests for the sake of that interest, not college entrance. They emphasized that authenticity is more important to the university than aiming for uniqueness as a goal unto itself.

To that end, don't homeschool your student because you think it will get her into a great school, and recognize that homeschooling will also not keep her from a great school.

Director Buckley gave further insight into this perspective: "I sit on the review committee for our honors college, and we see many homeschooled applicants. I hear a great deal from my colleagues about how great the students have been—the homeschool honor students, specifically. Many times homeschooled students come with a different level of discipline; they've had to learn to learn without having a teacher looking over their shoulders. Most of the homeschooled students we are seeing in honors are also students who have taken advantage of fine arts or athletics through their local school districts, and they often have college credits as incoming freshmen. There is a high acceptance rate of homeschoolers to our honors college. At times, I get an earful from advisors on all sorts of issues on campus. Nobody has ever come to me expressing any sort of concerns about admitting homeschoolers."

When asked about the number of homeschooled applicants, all four experts agreed that their numbers (ranging from a handful to low hundreds) are inaccurately low. "The incoming freshman class at Duke this year," Dean Guttentag noted, "has about a half dozen self-identified homeschool graduates. I suspect that number *significantly* undercounts the actual number of students with homeschool experience in their transcript somewhere. Unless students make a point of telling us they have been homeschooled somewhere along the way, we don't have any way of knowing unless they graduated from a pure homeschool high school environment."

When asked about how admissions officers perceive homeschooled applicants now, Dean Guttentag was quick to add: "There is a fluidity now in secondary education, with many hybrid learning models of online, virtual, distance, or homeschool learning—just to name a few—and admissions departments have begun to adapt evaluation criteria to reflect that diversity of learning experiences. We have discovered that very advanced students will often have a variety of learning modes to accelerate their education. We have also found that fluidity of education is a good thing—it reinforces the inclination of admissions officers to take a closer look at applicants as individuals, and prevents us from pigeon-holing students as historically admissions departments may have done."

The pigeon-holing Dean Guttentag referred to was consistently referenced by all our interviewees as having been a standard perspective in the past but no longer. Rather than viewing applicants as a continuation of a campus culture, admissions directors are eager to welcome students who reflect a perspective that may be alternative to others on campus, in order to provide a spectrum of opinions within student life that represents the world off campus.

Vice Provost Turner echoed this point: "When we get an application from a homeschooled student we very much try to put students first and try to understand who they are. 'Knowing students by name and story' is our unofficial motto. As an institution, we value diversity and students from different perspectives—we know that will require more on our part. In general, I find the profession has been very accepting and welcoming of homeschool applications."

After each of our experts had the opportunity to explain how admissions perspectives have changed over the last 30 to 40 years, we went on to ask each of them if there were any anecdotes or trends—either positive or negative—they could recall about formerly homeschooled students on campus as undergraduates now.

> Universities are now eager to consider candidates not *despite* their uniqueness but *because* of it.

Dean Guttentag added, "I can't think of a single time that someone has questioned or pointed to a homeschooled student as a negative contributor or source of a problem—and, as a Dean of Admissions, that's the sort of thing you are likely held responsible for and hear about."

Vice Provost Farmer responded, "It's been a while since we've looked at homeschoolers as a group—part of the reason is it's hard to actually group them together and make generalizations. There seem to be as many reasons for homeschooling as there are homeschoolers. We did a study on the performance of homeschoolers 10 years ago at UNC and we found that they thrive or struggle just as any student does in the university and, in a way, that is encouraging for us. Homeschooled students are heirs to the joys and heartaches of being a student as all students are. We have seen homeschooled students make Phi Beta Kappa, and most homeschooled students are thriving. What we have found is that, just like any of our other students, homeschooled students can jump in the river when the time comes and swim among the other fish and make their way downstream—and that's a great thing."

Since universities clearly welcome homeschooled applicants and seek creative ways to evaluate each student fairly as individuals no matter their education background, our next question asked what students (and their parents) should consider in advance in order to develop a student narrative that leads to a strong application. All four experts aligned across nine key points of advice.

LETTERS OF RECOMMENDATION

All the experts were keen to land on this point first, with the basic guidance that even if the parent is the primary teacher, applicants should look for letters of recommendation outside the home. While all agreed they accept whatever letters they receive in applications, they admitted that a letter from a parent is still a letter from a parent; it will reflect depth and nuances that another applicant's letter from a teacher never could. "We had about 205 homeschooled candidates apply this year and it would not surprise me if a third to half had letters from parents in their files," Vice Provost Farmer chuckled. "We're glad to receive them, but we read them as though we were writing them about our own children. And in a desire to measure similar qualities across all applications, it becomes difficult to compare letters when a parent knows the student far more intimately than a professional educator."

"If I had one piece of advice for homeschooled students, it would be to take advantage of your local community college."

It is not that the university doesn't trust parent letters, all were quick to emphasize. Rather, the parent recommendations included topics or variables that didn't exist in a traditional letter of recommendation and therefore could not be included in the evaluation across the board. "Even for parents with the best of intentions, their letters are full of depth, complexity, and nuance—and the problem isn't that parents share it; the problem is that we don't get that from other applications and therefore makes it difficult to compare with other applications to ensure an even playing field," Dean Guttentag clarified.

"Every student deserves to have teachers who love them, and so any letter we get from any teacher we hope is from someone who loves the candidate they are writing about," Vice Provost Farmer agreed. "It's just that the farther you get away from the blood relationship, the easier it is to hear what teachers are saying and not be required to filter it."

So who should students ask for a letter of recommendation? Experts agreed that the best case scenario was for the applicant to take a class outside the home that would enable the student to be evaluated by an independent teacher—someone who could compare that student to his peers. Beyond that, other alternatives are employers or supervisors. All the experts encouraged students to avoid letters of recommendation from anyone they pay directly (such as a tutor or music teacher) because that layer of complexity makes it harder to evaluate. If a student wants to ask someone in the community for a recommendation (such as a scout leader, coach, or youth pastor), experts agreed that it was fine but not as ideal as the first scenario. As Director Buckley pointed out, "We use letters of recommendation as an opportunity to press us into a 'yes' if we are considering saying 'no.'" Given that, choose wisely.

OUTSIDE EVALUATION

Similar to seeking out a letter of recommendation from a teacher outside the home, our experts suggested that homeschooled students pursue a couple of external courses that would enable them to be graded and evaluated by a non-relative. Whether it is a class at a community college, a co-op, or a local school, the various admissions directors agreed that it was worth the extra effort for the applicant to prove she was capable of thriving in a classroom environment less customized than what homeschooling might offer. In addition, this is a great place for the student to develop necessary skills for college that may not be readily used in her homeschool environment, such as note taking, managing external deadlines, or regular and diverse types of testing. "If I had one piece of advice for homeschooled students, it would be to take advantage of your local community college, because then we know what we're getting when we look at your transcript," commented Director Buckley.

COLLABORATION WITH PEERS

Even though concerns about homeschoolers and socialization continue to diminish with time, admissions directors still noted that it was worth pursuing activities, employment, volunteer work, or sports that show the applicant is capable of collaborating with peers. "Collaboration is a big part of our campus life," Vice Provost Turner offered, "and how that translates to admissions is making sure students are well-prepared and give evidence of spending time working in groups alongside their peers."

Dean Guttentag leaned into this point further, clarifying how it is key to the admissions process: "There are at least two communities that every student is joining at college—an academic community and a personal/social community—and when we make admissions decisions, we think about both of those and what the applicant will contribute. Homeschoolers are not absolved of showing what kind of community member they would be simply by fact they are not in a traditional secondary school community."

COMMUNITY COLLEGE CREDITS

If you decide to have your student take courses at the community college, do so knowing it will certainly expand his knowledge, strengthen his skills as a student, and provide outside evaluation of his work beyond home. With all that in mind, understand that the credits may not count toward a college degree unless there is a direct agreement between the community college and a state university. Vice Provost Turner emphasized this: "We regularly get a number of students who have earned credit at community colleges while in high school. The coursework may help place you in the proper level of class in college, but it will not replace your college class. That's something that has been disappointing for homeschooled students especially, so it's important to make that clear."

DECREASE BARRIERS TO ENTRY

The smart college applicant is one who makes it as easy as possible for the admissions officer to say "yes." With that in mind, experts agreed that applicants are wise to decrease barriers to entry by including easily recognizable scoring methods as proof of their academic preparation.

"Colleges want a sense of the academic preparation of a student," Dean Guttentag said, "such as Cambridge curriculum, AP, and IB which are all helpful identifiers because of their fixed syllabus, consistent assessment, and comparative nature across schools. For homeschool students who may not access those types of advanced-level courses, we encourage SAT subject tests and AP exams, which help us assess how much the student has learned. I would encourage homeschool families to think about reducing the number of obstacles to entry, which in their specific case is unknown variables. Because we cannot reference their high school of origin, more work may be needed on the part of that student to educate us about his or her own unique education." Even online coursework completed at respected institutions would validate the applicant's role as student.

Director Buckley does not expect this will come as a surprise to homes-chooling parents. "Overall, I think that parents who choose to homeschool know generally how colleges are going to look at their child's application, and antici-pate that extra work will be required on their part. They are careful to make sure the rigor is there, usually do their research, and don't leave anything to chance for their student. I have found that homeschool parents are self-aware. If they have the means to do test prep or independent counselors, they will."

CONSIDER ALTERNATIVE LEARNING OPPORTUNITIES

One suggestion shared by Director Buckley caught Sue's attention—the notion of students attending university summer camps prior to applying to college. "Expe-rience at college camps on an application always helps us because the student is clearly doing academic work, it addresses a well-rounded social component, and it shows they have passion in a subject area. It makes us want them to come dig into that subject area with us. If a student has participated in a marine biology camp, we think they would be successful here at our university because we can build on that. Many of these camps have scholarships or waivers, so if it seems unaffordable there may still be a way."

> The smart college applicant is one who makes it easy for the admissions officer to say "yes."

DO YOUR RESEARCH

If you are planning to homeschool your student through high school, it is worth reaching out to admissions offices at colleges you think your student might want to consider *prior to beginning her freshman year of high school*. (Yes, this is planning four years ahead.) Our experts noted that many admissions offices nationwide now have staff dedicated to helping homeschooled applicants. First, the experts recommended looking at the university's admissions web page to see if there is information directed at homeschool applicants. Beyond that, they encouraged parents to call and ask about accredited curriculums that would be known and respected by the university, should the student decide to apply there in the future. Not all universities have the same list, but there is likely to be some overlap.

In addition, experts encouraged students to engage early (as in, years early) in the admissions process. Vice Provost Farmer specified: "We don't expect parents to shove their 14-year-old into the admissions office to ask all the right questions on the first go around, but there is also a way to support the student so that the parent doesn't dominate the conversation but instead helps her find her voice and learn some things about herself that she wouldn't have if parents directed the conversation. I don't think homeschool parents are different from any other parent that way, of seeking the balance between support and release."

Furthermore, the experts encouraged parents to reach out to their regional admissions officers at the beginning of their student's high school career, to ask questions about accreditation and how they can make it easy to evaluate and measure their student's progress. (Note: You are not asking for the secret formula that gets your child into the university; you are asking for suggestions of additional background or experience it would be helpful to provide when applying.)

> "Find the admissions officer responsible for your territory and engage with that person."

Vice Provost Turner's next bit of advice took me completely by surprise: "Find the admissions officer responsible for your territory and engage with that person. It establishes a relationship and interest in the university early on, and will give you an opportunity to learn from that university's perspective how you should approach the process. University admissions offices are often eager to engage—most people don't realize that we are happy to do so." She was right: It was news to me. I had always assumed that the identity of the admissions officer was secret; the process had a hint of mystery. But all the experts encouraged students to reach out to their admissions offices and officers early on.

Before doing so, however—to the extent you can—anticipate the need of the admissions officer. "I think it's important for homeschool parents to enter imaginatively into the lives of admissions officers—just as it is important for admissions officers to enter imaginatively into the lives and circumstances of applicants. It is not only the gracious thing to do, it is helpful and smart," counseled Vice Provost Farmer. "We had 45,000 people who applied for admission this year, and we try our best to understand everything we can about them. But we do have limits on our time. If parents can appreciate that in advance and help us by providing context—or encourage their students to provide context by pursuing learning outside the home and to give us that peer context—that is the generous and helpful thing for them to do. It is also the smart thing for them to do because it increases the chances we will understand the student fairly and make a reasonable decision."

This was another point the admissions directors reiterated: Lean into individual passions and interests. Too often, they admitted, it was clear when a student had joined Chess Club because she thought it made her look smart (even though she didn't like chess), or he joined the dance team because he thought it would make him stand out (even though his heart wasn't in it). After reading thousands upon thousands of applications, year after year, our experts emphasized that a student's genuine passion and interest in an area becomes apparent quickly versus those who are just checking boxes. If you are fascinated by hydroponics, go for it! Want to program a Raspberry Pi? Please do. Pursue what excites you, because you will be more likely to excel in that passion and present the best elements of who you are.

As this applies specifically to homeschoolers, Dean Guttentag noted an application issue his department typically does *not* see from homeschoolers: "One advantage we see with homeschooled applicants is a much lower mental barrier. What I mean by that is homeschooled students don't need to overcome the same external peer pressures that might influence what matters to them or where to put their time. Coming out of middle school, most students want to be either invisible or alpha, so the advantage for the homeschooler is eliminating that mental barrier when asking the question, 'What matters to you and what are you going to do about it?' In a funny way, homeschoolers are at an advantage because they don't have to worry about the culture of their school and extra-curricular selection based on peer bias. Homeschoolers tend to choose what matters to them."

So use your flexible lifestyle of learning to expose your student to unique environments, such as internships or unusual job opportunities. Encourage your student to pursue her passions and develop an interesting narrative about herself—not just for a college application, but because she is developing something far more important. She is developing the adult she hopes to become.

Again, after reading countless applications, the experts tell us they can spot a shrug from a coverup. If a student has made a misstep somewhere along the way, rather than the university finding out about it on their own and dismissing the student's application for lack of character, they would rather the student own the mistake honestly and explain how future choices will be better.

Everyone makes mistakes—owning up to them takes strength and integrity. I had a brilliant friend growing up, and both of us decided to apply to the same university. At the time of writing his application, he was temporarily suspended from high school—so he wrote about it in his application essay. Not only did he get accepted (and to a number of other elite universities), he got accepted knowing they respected him for his whole, true story.

Twenty years after that story, Dean Guttentag seconds the point: "High school students should not do what they think people like us want solely because they think we want it. Their applications will ring with a dissonance that is not authentic. What we want are students who say, 'This is who I am, this is what matters to me, these are the choices I have made, you either like me or you don't, but I'm not going to try to be something I am not in the hopes you will like me better.'"

> "We aren't going to hold students to some impossible pre-pandemic standard."

Vice Provost Farmer addressed the same principle from a different perspective: "I have some advice about what I hope students won't do. I hope they won't try to be the same as everyone else. Let's say one family's choice of homeschooling was because they wanted their children to spend more time together, to take more responsibility for each other so that they emerge from adolescence with a different kind of relationship than the one they would have had if they hadn't been homeschooled. I think it is good for a student in that circumstance, whose life has been built around the home, to come to us and talk about looking after younger siblings and chores as an extracurricular and as something that is important to him. It is who the student is and who we hope will come to us—not a student trying to hack off an appendage or grow a limb in order to look like everybody else. I hope students generally do what is best for themselves, making them smarter and healthier. This will not only help them develop a sense of themselves, it will prepare them to make the difference they are called to make in the world."

COVID-19 AND BEYOND

Now more than ever, parents are asking, "If I decide to homeschool my student through COVID-19, will that negatively impact his chances of getting into college?" Frankly, it's one of the questions that not only inspired the timing of this chapter but of this entire book—the aim of homeschooling with excellence so that students *do* have options at the end of their journey. Each of the experts we spoke to had closing thoughts to offer on this subject.

"COVID is calling on admissions officers to be flexible and focus on student preparedness and academic strength in a new way," Vice Provost Turner asserted. "Whatever preparation we have had in evaluating homeschool students over the years has certainly informed us as we look for creative ways to evaluate future candidates whose transcripts are impacted by school disruption as it relates to COVID. If there are families out there considering homeschooling who have the ability to do so, we respect that. There are all kinds of ways to learn, and colleges need to do a better job respecting people coming from all kinds of academic backgrounds."

But what about the global fear of our children falling behind? What about worries of a generation who lost a year or more of education and what that will mean for their futures? How can parents possibly prepare their students for a future none of us can envision? Vice Provost Farmer's words were compelling, encouraging, and reassuring for parents everywhere as we make the best decisions we can for our children during COVID-19.

"In light of COVID and the challenges families face with education, I hope they realize we are thinking about them. Our hearts go out to people. Five years from now, when students apply to college, we aren't going to forget that today happened. We aren't going to forget there was a pandemic. We know that all students everywhere are being shaped by these difficult circumstances, and that every family is making the best choices they can. We are not going to forget that. We don't know what we are going to do with what we know because we haven't gotten there yet, but we aren't going to forget what families have gone through. And I hope that takes a little of the pressure off. We aren't going to hold students to some impossible pre-pandemic standard. We will remember this time and I hope that we will have the humanity to try to understand the choices parents made and the impact that had on students.

"Having said all that," he continued, "I think happy students learn and grow more. I hope that as parents are making choices they will focus not only on what they are doing to position their children to be happy when they are 25 or 45, but positioning them for what they need to be happy right now. For some students, that might be going back to school even if there is a risk. For others, it might be that they really need to be learning with their parents.

"My personal experience with parenting is that it is one long exercise of hoping against hope and having faith. I hope parents will have faith that the decisions they are making with best intentions around the wellbeing of their children will lead to the best possible result down the road, whatever that result might be."

Let it be.

15

But What If I Want to Send My Child Back to School?

Transitioning Back Into Traditional Education

A s by now you have read countless times in this book (I can't help but reiterate it one last time for our final chapter!): Yours is not mine. Your students are not my students, your schedule is not my schedule, your timing is not my timing. Every family has its own plan for education. Choosing to educate your child at home K–12 does not make you a better parent than choosing to homeschool for one year, or even not at all. What matters is that you make the best decision you can for your family and for each of your children as needed.

For our family, we decided to homeschool K–8 (though, admittedly, that is just a template; I am still homeschooling three of our four children at the time of writing this, so that may change as we become more aware of their needs as time goes on). Based on our experiences in college, my husband and I wanted to give our children the opportunity to spread their wings at home while we could still provide support and guidance, prior to them moving anywhere in the country after high school to pursue college or life more independently.

In addition, we have chosen to expose our children to a public school education at a high school with excellent academic resources so that they can explore some of life's big topics alongside peers and teachers with a different world-view—with the intent, again, that we can provide support and guidance for those conversations at the end of each day at home. Because we don't know where each of our children is headed in life, Josh and I want to provide an education that extends beyond academics, character growth, and extracurriculars to learning how to engage meaningfully and thoughtfully with our culture.

Now you see why I reiterated one of my favorite points: This is just our family's take on things. Your family may have a completely different view—choosing a shorter or longer homeschool model—and I respect that. I trust that as parents we are all aiming to do what is best for our children and our families.

When my oldest child was in third grade, my publisher reached out, asking me to write a book on homeschooling. I declined, saying I wanted a few more years in the lab; I wanted to experience the transition from as many angles as possible, especially guiding at least one of our own children through the transition process, so I could provide parents with the most practical advice possible.

So here we are: My son is moving into his sophomore year after a successful first year of high school, and after interviewing experts and experienced homeschool parents alike, I am equipped to give you some important tools for transitioning your child into traditional school at any grade.

As you think about the possibility of preparing your student for mainstream education (K–12), this chapter outlines what I experienced as a student who transitioned out of homeschooling, what I experienced as a professional educator transitioning homeschoolers onto our campus, what I experienced as a parent transitioning our eldest into the local public school—and, most important, what I have learned from interviewing almost 100 experienced homeschool parents, school guidance counselors, principals, and professional educators about making this transition as smooth as possible.

PLAN AHEAD

The overarching message for this entire lesson is to plan ahead as much as you possibly can. Certainly, there are scenarios in life where that is not possible—the resources here will still be helpful; modify and apply them as best as you can. In addition, as this book is being written during COVID-19, recognize that, coming out of the pandemic, school systems will likely be more accustomed to transitioning homeschoolers back into the mainstream; as a result, much of this process will become even easier.

BE PROACTIVE

Most of what this chapter covers is ideal for students transitioning into junior high or high school, though it can easily be applied to elementary, as well. A year and a half prior to enrolling your homeschooled student in a traditional school, be proactive and set up a meeting with a guidance counselor at that school.

During that meeting, ask open-ended questions such as, "How can I make it easier for you to place my student in the appropriate classes when she enrolls in a year and a half?" Especially at the high school level, some schools prefer that homeschooled students enroll with an accredited math class in their background to help identify accurate placement.

And every high school has its own order for math classes. Some offer Algebra 1, Algebra 2, then Geometry. Others offer Algebra 1, Geometry, then Algebra 2. (Our school divides Geometry in half and puts half of it in a year with Algebra 1 and the other half in the year with Algebra 2, which is a new trend.) Whatever the school's order, you will want to do your best to prepare and align your student ahead of time.

By meeting with the counselor at school this far in advance, you'll have plenty of time to prepare for their requirements and develop a portfolio to prove what is needed to get your student into the appropriate class. It also develops a positive working relationship with the counseling office from the start, showing that you are an attentive parent looking to adapt yourself to the school versus the other way around. (There will be time later to ask the school to accommodate your student, if needed.)

> A year and a half prior to enrolling in a traditional school, be proactive and set up a meeting with the guidance counselor.

Beyond working directly with the new school, prepare your student for a traditional classroom by enrolling him in a local co-op or community class that has deadlines, tests, and basic classroom structures that will be an easy warm-up to a traditional classroom setting.

In addition, seek ways to get your student socially engaged, either on the new campus or at the feeder campus to the new school through sports teams or other extracurriculars. This will give your student the opportunity to acclimate gently into her new world and develop a social base of friends and familiar faces so the halls feel like a friendly place on her first day of school.

COORDINATE

The January before starting school, coordinate with the counselor to bring your student in to meet all together. (For this first meeting, my son baked chocolate chip cookies and delivered them, still warm, to the guidance office receptionist and his counselor as a thank you for doing the extra work of getting him enrolled into the system. It's a great idea to start off this relationship with gratitude, recognizing that it *does* require extra work for the staff to get new students enrolled. Yes, it is part of their job, but that doesn't mean we can't show appreciation.

If your student has unique education needs, this is a great time to work out those details and to find out when class registration begins for the fall. From there, ask the counselor if you can arrange a time for your child to tour campus or potentially shadow a student for a day to get accustomed to the space. Some high schools are now offering special orientation nights for incoming freshmen or transfer students the spring before they arrive on campus, so ask if your school has any sort of welcome event planned. It's ideal, once your student has her schedule for the fall, to get permission to walk through her classroom locations a day or two before school starts and practice opening her locker, if she has one. (Again, coming out of COVID-19, I suspect transitioning into traditional education will likely become more normalized in our schools.)

KEEP RECORDS

Records are simply a way of showing progress and accountability. Even if the school doesn't require you to provide them, I still recommend it. When it came time to enroll our son in classes for his freshman year, we came in with a portfolio of work samples that included an essay, poetry, a science experiment write-up, and his recent national exam scores. The counselor was hugely grateful, and it immediately validated our requests to place him in specific classes.

If you need to advocate for accommodations or a specialized lesson plan, consider including those records in the file as well, since that may impact course selection. Or if you suspect that your student may need an Individualized Education Plan (IEP) or other classroom modifications due to an undiagnosed learning need, this is a great time to ask the counselor how to look into evaluating those needs and getting them met.

STUDY SKILLS

Make sure your student has sound study skills, whether in fourth grade or heading into college. Find a book, class, or resource, such as *Study Smart, Study Less* (which can be applied to all grade levels), that will help your student identify his learning preferences, develop some flexible structures as a professional student, and apply his strengths to his homework routine in order to succeed in class.

In order to launch into traditional school, your student at every level past third grade should know how to take notes, prepare for a test, manage time, and keep a student calendar. If your student needs test prep skills, consider finding a tutor to teach her the basics.

CONFIRM THE CORE

The summer before your student transitions into traditional education is a great time to confirm her core knowledge. Check out books that summarize key content points in core subject areas that are specific to her grade level before transitioning. That way, you are certain she has all her bases covered and she can focus in the fall on acclimating to school rather than catching up on forgotten subject matter.

In addition to core knowledge, confirm your student's social core by registering him for a fall sports team or another large activity club that will get him on campus a few days before school starts to get to know other students. Beyond school clubs, look for groups in the community the summer prior—such as volunteer clubs, gym groups, community center groups, church youth groups, or ways to hang out with friends in the neighborhood—that have a nexus of similarly aged students who may be attending your child's school.

We intentionally invested time the summer before school started helping our eldest develop a social network that gave him the opportunity to meet students attending his high school through various groups and teams. We made it a goal to help him know at least a few other freshmen before he walked on campus.

Once the school year began, we encouraged him to pursue a few clubs on campus to get involved and make friends more easily. He chose the mock trial team, swim team, and computer programming competitions, and all three went a long way toward helping him feel like he had a place on campus.

ENGAGE EARLY

Look for ways as a parent in the new school to engage on campus over the summer or early in the fall. There are a lot of ways parents can support their schools as volunteers. Schools often need help cleaning the campus grounds before fall begins, and I can tell you from experience teachers always appreciate help getting gum off the bottom of desks.

The counseling center often welcomes parent volunteers to proctor exams, coach in the futures program, or chaperone events. It's meaningful as a parent to begin to serve the staff and teachers who will be impacting your student's life so you can stay connected to what is happening in her new world on campus.

Beyond being available on campus, make a point of contacting your student's school counselor once a quarter—ideally in person—to discuss how your child is managing the transition and stay ahead of any needs. It's critical to continue to advocate on behalf of your student if you sense additional support may be needed, and most likely your school will be eager to help.

THE LAUNCH

Our job as parents is to prepare, protect, provide for, and eventually launch our children into their futures. How you choose to educate your child is up to you and your child's needs.

Each of our children are different; how I educate one may not look like how I educate the others. Our goal is to take into account the needs of each of our kids as well as the needs of our family when making that decision. Both matter.

And if we have done our job as parent teachers well, our children will launch bravely into their bright futures, able to apply all those great life principles we have learned together.

Appendix

Team Crossman: Chores

DISHES & CLEAN KITCHEN

- All food away
- Counters tidied and wiped
- No trash
- Leftover dishes rinsed and stacked in sink

If dishes are not done by time deadline, you must do next meal too. (Parents reserve the right to rescind for extenuating circumstances).

Breakfast	Lunch	Dinner
EVELYN (Done by 10am)	**ISAIAH** (Done by 2pm)	**JOSIAH & EVANGELINE**

JOSIAH	ISAIAH	EVELYN	EVANGELINE
• Team Laundry (fold & away) • Set Table (nightly) • Trash/Recycle: Take out without being asked, includes trash day • Tidy Car (THU)	• Vacuum: Every night hardwoods; carpets (MON) • Mom Helper (ask!) • Organize Helper (TUES/THU) • Sister Helper: With love; includes supervising bird	• Dog: Scoop & feed (daily), bathe (SUN/THU) • Deck/Porch Tidy: Sweep (TUE) • Windows: Clean dog smudges (MON) • Tidy Commons & PR (Daily)	• Library Books: Organize & bag • Lysol handles & switches (TUE) • T.P. in all bathrooms (MON) • Clean ½ bath (THU)

Age Appropriate Chores

Consider these possibilities of how to develop autonomy, confidence, and independence through chores with your children. Because children develop at different speeds, this is simply a general guideline: parents should supervise and apply their best judgment.

AGES 2-3

PERSONAL CHORES

- Clean bedroom by categories
  (i.e. books, trash, dirty clothes, toys, etc.)
- Put toys downstairs where they go
- Line up shoes by the back door
- Dictate thank you notes

TEAM CHORES

- Fold washcloths
- Sweep the front steps
- Fill pet's water bowl
- Dust
- Pick up trash inside and outside
- Organize library books on shelf
- Help set table
- Empty plastics from dishwasher

AGES 4-5

PERSONAL CHORES

- Get dressed (prearrange drawers for
  easy access and obvious seasonal selection)
- Make bed
- Clean under bed
- Organize bookshelf neatly
- Make easy snacks
- Sort clean laundry in piles by type
  (don't worry about folding)
- Color pictures as thank you notes

TEAM CHORES

- Feed pets
- Carry things from car to house
- Empty silverware from dishwasher
- Clear table
- Sweep under table
- Match socks
- Water plants
- Weed garden
- Help younger siblings
- Scrub cabinets or floorboards with
  soapy sponge
- Wipe handles and switches with baby wipes

AGES 6-7

PERSONAL CHORES
- Make bed daily
- Clean room daily
- Put own laundry away
- Brush teeth after meals
- Style own hair in morning
- Pick weather-appropriate outfit
- Write thank you notes
- Pack lunch or snack
- Pack for sports practice using a list
- Help sort own laundry into washer
- Strip sheets off the bed

TEAM CHORES
- Wet-mop floors
- Vacuum
- Help prepare food
- Empty indoor trash
- Answer phone with manners
- Greet and dismiss guests at
  door with manners
- Exercise pet within the house/yard
- Empty whole dishwasher (except knives;
  glassware on counter if too high)
- Rake leaves
- Peel vegetables
- Wipe handles/sinks/switches with
  disinfectant wipes and gloves
- Collect mail
- Clean windows/mirrors with glass cleaner
- Collect garbage
- Read aloud to siblings
- Fold rags and towels
- Replace batteries

AGES 8-9

PERSONAL CHORES
- All personal hygiene
- Use alarm clock
- Responsible for own homework (finish lesson)
- Responsible for library card and account
- Get own sports gear ready for practice
  without help
- Do own laundry
- Apply basic first aid
- Put sheets on bed
- Manage personal items (like charging devices)
- Save money without supervision

TEAM CHORES
- Remember family birthdays
- Keep track of calendar events
- Prepare easy meals
- Wash dishes
- Empty dishwasher
- Sterilize kitchen counters
- Take trash to curb and back
- Sterilize bathroom counters
- Clean toilet
- Wipe floors
- Sweep porch

AGES 10-11

PERSONAL CHORES
- Manage your weekly laundry cycle
- Write invitations
- Balance bank account
- Donate to charity
- Communicate between coaches/teachers and parents

TEAM CHORES
- Wash dog
- Put groceries away
- Vacuum car
- Learn deep cleaning
- Change light bulbs
- Clean tub/shower
- Wash family car

AGES 12+

PERSONAL CHORES
- Communicate schedule in advance
- Manage time
- Complete work before play without supervision
- Mend clothes
- Invest savings

TEAM CHORES
- Mow lawn
- Snow blow driveway
- Assist in large yard work projects
- Iron clothes
- Watch younger siblings
- Make balanced family meals
- Paint
- Help with simple home repairs *(using tools like a drill, hammer, wrench, screwdrivers, and allen wrench)*
- Clean out refrigerator

Other Books
By Anne Crossman

STUDY SMART, STUDY LESS

This witty, straight-forward, illustrated guide teaches students how to study using their strengths. Using the best research on memory, as well as practical tips that have been tested in classrooms worldwide, this book equips students to learn study habits that get fast results, discover their study persona, earn better grades, and get higher test scores. By learning how to learn, students will not only feel smarter, they'll be smarter.

GETTING THE BEST OUT OF COLLEGE

For undergrads (and parents) wanting their tuition to pay off, *Getting The Best Out of College* is a must-read. Distilling over fifty years of experience from leading minds at top tier institutions, it reveals insider advice that makes the hefty price tag worthwhile: how to impress professors, pick the best courses (and do well in them), design a meaningful transcript, earn remarkable internships, prepare for a successful career, and more.

TRYING TO REMEMBER

A tribute to victims of Alzheimer's Disease and their families, *Trying to Remember* is a memoir of one family's struggle with Alzheimer's, using poems to create snapshots of the collection of moments that lead to goodbye. Using simple, heart-felt language, Crossman addresses some of the greater griefs of Alzheimer's head on, finding a way to say goodbye with hope. "...And if I wait to say so long/for when it's truly time,/what if you're already gone/and we don't say goodbye?"

Praise for Previous Books

A refreshing, smart, and useful guide to college that should be basic required reading for incoming freshmen everywhere.

BOB WOODWARD, Pulitzer Prizewinning Journalist (GTBOC)

If you read this book and take the counsel it offers seriously, you will be better prepared for success. I hope you will read this book and get the most out of it—and let it help you get the best out of college.

MIKE "COACH K" KRZYZEWSKI, Head Coach Duke Men's Basketball Team and USA National Team (GTBOC)

Anne Crossman demystifies studying, proving that academic success isn't magic...her book is accessible and helpful for ALL students, particularly those transitioning to high school. Parents, teachers, and counselors who want to help their kids succeed would also do well to read it.

BRIAN COOPER, Director of Educational Programs, Duke University Talent Identification Program (SSSL)

Calling all teenagers (and their exasperated parents)! If you spend hours 'studying' without seeing your grades improve, are realizing that acting too cool for school isn't cool at all, or want to do better in school while gaining a sense of self (and a social life) this is the book for you.

GINGER FAY, Former Duke University Admissions Officer (SSSL)

Trying to Remember is a powerful and timely book. It will be a permanent part of the literature of Alzheimer's disease. Like all good books, and especially this one, it is against forgetting.

THOMAS LUX, Author of *God Particles* (TTR)

Made in the USA
Monee, IL
24 June 2021

72233618R00134